ISRAEL
for
Christians

ISRAEL
for
Christians

A. JAMES RUDIN

FORTRESS PRESS   Philadelphia

Library of Congress Cataloging in Publication Data

Rudin, A. James (Arnold James), 1934–
   Israel for Christians.

   1. Israel.   2. Jewish-Arab relations.   3. Judaism—
Relations—Christianity—1945– . 4. Christianity
and other religions—Judaism—1945– . I. Title.
DS126.5.R85   956.94   82–7241
ISBN 0–8006–1643–X   AACR2

9590E82   Printed in the United States of America   1–1643

This book is lovingly dedicated

to Philip and Beatrice,
who first taught me about the Wall . . .

to Marcia, Eve, and Jennifer,
who made it to the Wall with me . . .

and to the memory of Bert,
who sadly never got there . . .

Acknowledgments

I am grateful to Norman Hjelm and Harold Rast of Fortress Press who encouraged and supported me in this project. Berenice Hoffman gave important assistance and guidance. Thanks also go to my colleagues Judith Banki, Inge Lederer Gibel, Florence Mordhorst, Zachariah Shuster, and Marc Tanenbaum for their contributions. Finally, the American Jewish Committee provided a sabbatical leave that enabled me to visit Israel to pursue my research. However, the views and opinions expressed in this book are my own, and do not necessarily reflect those of the AJC.

Contents

Introduction

Since 1968 my professional responsibilities have brought me into close personal relationships with much of the organized Christian community. In my many meetings and dialogues with Christians, one word always evokes more emotion and passion than any other. That word is "Israel." The reemergence of an independent Jewish state onto the world stage in 1948 has compelled Christians and Jews to examine themselves and each other in a new light. Whenever Christians and Jews meet, Israel is at the center of the encounter, but sadly Israel is often a cause of misunderstanding and even hostility between the two groups.

Over and over again, I have met thoughtful Christians who confessed how little they actually know about the state of Israel: its origins, its purpose, its people, its problems, and its hopes. Even though the Middle East is one of the most documented and reported subjects in the world today (as I quickly discovered during the writing of this book!), many Christians have unfortunately gained limited knowledge either from authors who refuse to accept the legitimacy and permanence of the Jewish state or from authors who make exclusive apocalyptic Christian theological claims for Israel. Neither view is helpful in gaining a balanced and accurate picture of modern Israel. Nor can the news media reports that are always constrained by the pressures of deadlines and fast-moving events provide an adequate answer to the oft-asked question: "Why is there an Israel?" This book is my response to that query.

But more than a "description" of Israel is needed; a "prescription" for action is also required. Hopefully, this book will aid Christians not only to understand Israel, but will offer ways to advance the cause of a just and lasting peace between Israel and its neighbors. Why a book about Israel? The Prophet Isaiah has provided the mandate:

For Zion's sake will I not hold my peace,
And for Jerusalem's sake I will not rest ... (62:1, *KJV*).

As this book went to press, two important events took place in the Middle East. First, although Israel dealt the Palestine Liberation Organization a major military defeat in Lebanon, the PLO still remains a significant political and diplomatic force, one that has not abandoned the overall goals of its charter. Second, the Beirut massacre of Palestinians by Lebanese Christian militias shocked the entire world. Because Israeli troops were in Beirut at the time, the Israeli public successfully demanded the creation of an impartial national commission of inquiry. Even though Israel is a full-fledged functioning democracy, the Israeli people's response was, nonetheless, extraordinary, and involved all segments of the society, especially the press and the army.

1 | *Israel Is Real*

There is a small crowded shop on a Jerusalem main street that offers its customers a wide assortment of lettered T-shirts. Some shirts prominently display the faces of famous rock musical performers. Other brightly colored shirts boldly feature comic-strip characters or witty bons mots. Yet the best selling T-shirt has only three words imprinted across its front: "Israel Is Real"—a proud, almost defiant, declaration.

Why have so many people purchased a shirt that simply proclaims such an obvious truth? Why has the semantically clever phrase "Israel Is Real" struck such a responsive chord? It is, after all, a statement that hardly needs to be made since the reality of Israel can be experienced and understood in an extraordinary number of ways.

One way to experience Israel is to visit the country; Israel is real on the most obvious and natural level. It has its own national language, Hebrew; it effectively controls its sovereign territory. Israel issues its own passports, visas, and currency; it maintains its own governmental, legal, and military institutions, and it provides for the health, education, welfare, and security of its 3.9 million citizens. Israel has its own national airline and merchant marine fleet, and it carries on diplomatic relations with many nations of the world including its Arab neighbor, Egypt. Israel exercises all the functions of an independent modern nation-state, including the right to disagree publicly with its friends as well as with its adversaries. But all of these signs of nationhood do not begin to exhaust the reality that is Israel.

Another reality is the memory of the intense struggle to achieve Israeli independence. Since the end of World War II in 1945, over 100 new states have gained political independence, an unprecedented explosion and assertion of national sovereignty. Many of these new states were once part of vast European and American colonial empires that were located in Asia, Africa, and South America. Fired by the twin ideas of national liberation and political self-determination, such diverse states as India, Pakistan, Ghana, Barbados, Guyana, Zimbabwe, and Israel have all attained independence from British rule since 1945. During the same period Indonesia freed itself from Holland; Angola from Portugal; Zaire from Belgium; Syria, Lebanon, Algeria, and Vietnam from France. The Philippine Islands achieved its independence from the United States as well.

These examples are part of a dynamic global decolonization process that is not yet complete. New independent nation-states emerge each year to take their place both as members of the United Nations and as new additions in rapidly expanding postage-stamp albums. Israel's independence, coming in 1948, was one of the earliest successful national liberation movements following World War II.

Today the basic facts about Israel's independence make for almost prosaic reading. The land of Israel* has passed through many foreign rulers and powers since biblical times, and all the occupying forces left their mark, for good or ill, upon the land. Shortly after the collapse of the Christian Crusader rule in 1187, a militarily powerful group of professional soldiers and former slaves of the Arab rulers of Baghdad gained control of the land of Israel. These non-Arab Muslims, called "Mamelukes" (the Arabic word for "owned" or "possessed"), were mainly Tartars, Mongols, and Kurds from Central Asia. They ruled from 1250 until the even more powerful Ottoman Turkish empire, also non-Arab Muslims, conquered the land in 1517. That rule ended in 1917 when Great Britain captured the region during World War I, and following its victory, the London government was awarded a League of Nations mandate over the land of Israel, then called Palestine.

In 1947 the United Nations General Assembly voted for a partition plan that provided for a Jewish state and an Arab state in man-

---

*The various names given to the land clearly reveal the many political, religious, and social forces that have been at work during the last thirty-five hundred years: Canaan, Israel, Judea, Palestine, South Syria, the Promised Land, and the Holy Land. The traditional Jewish name for the area is *Eretz Israel*, the land of Israel, or simply *Ha-Aretz*, the land. The author will follow this practice except when other names are historically relevant or necessary.

date Palestine. The Jewish leadership accepted the plan; the Arabs did not. The partition vote was extraordinary in that the two superpowers, the United States and the Soviet Union, jointly supported the UN proposal.

The British mandate terminated on May 14, 1948 and the state of Israel came into existence, its independence proclaimed by the leaders of the Jewish community in Palestine. For Jews it was the fulfillment of a dream that was thousands of years old: the physical return of the Jewish people to their national and spiritual homeland.

Yet the birth process of a human being is never simple, predictable, or painless; neither is the birth process of a nation. Few, if any, nation-states are "immaculately conceived" or peacefully born. Like so many other nations, an independent Israel came into the world amidst war, pain, blood, invasion, and agony, as well as with an inner strength and a collective will to survive.

Such birth pangs are rarely pretty, pure, or precise, but they are, nonetheless, real and authentic for the men and women and for the nations that experience them. Indeed, the actions and policies that were necessary to achieve independence are usually celebrated by later generations as sacred, almost mystical events in a nation's historical consciousness and self-understanding. It matters little, if at all, that such events were often acts of rebellion that were carried out against the ruling authority of the time.

Israel's battle to gain political independence followed this pattern. However, some additional and unique factors were also present. Most national liberation movements confront only one hostile power or regime, but the Jews of Palestine in the twentieth century faced two very different and difficult adversaries: the British mandate rule and the Arab leadership of the Middle East. Most national liberation movements successfully overthrow the ruling power when the subject people are politically united and reside together in large numbers; a "critical mass" is always deemed necessary by the historians of such movements. Neither factor was present when Israel became an independent state in 1948.

The Jewish people lacked political unity both in Palestine and throughout the world, and only six hundred and fifty thousand Jews lived in the land at the time. Nowhere in the Jewish Diaspora (the

Jewish communities living outside the land of Israel) did the Zionist movement have a majority of the Jewish community enrolled as active members.

Although the Zionist idea of returning the Jewish people to its ancient homeland originated in biblical times and was kept alive for thousands of years, it was not until 1897 that the movement became an active force in both Jewish and general history. In that year a bearded and charismatic thirty-seven-year-old Viennese Jewish journalist and playwright, Theodor Herzl, convened the first world Zionist Congress. As with many other national liberation movements, the Zionist Congress was forced to meet outside of the homeland. The ruling Ottoman Turks would not have permitted such a gathering in the land of Israel, and Herzl's dramatic call for political action primarily energized and excited the persecuted Jewish masses of Eastern Europe. The Congress met in neutral Basel, Switzerland, and it publicly called for the creation of a Jewish state in Palestine "secured by public law." A year earlier, in 1896, Herzl had published a slim pamphlet in German entitled *Der Judenstaat* in which he outlined his goal of achieving national Jewish independence. Herzl, with his majestic biblical appearance and his extraordinary gift for leadership, was revered by those Jews who were the victims of anti-Semitic acts in czarist Russia and other East European countries.

But Herzl's wild and extravagant dream of a Jewish state was ridiculed and fiercely attacked by some Jews in Western Europe and in the United States who were well acculturated to their various countries of residence and citizenship. Herzl's call for a return to Zion seemed both impossible to attain and hopelessly out of touch with the realities of enlightened life in the late nineteenth century. For such anti-Zionist Jews, Judaism was solely a religious identification. The last independent Jewish state or commonwealth had ended in A.D. 70 with the Roman capture of Jerusalem and the destruction of the Holy Temple. Although pious prayers for a physical restoration to Zion had been invoked for over eighteen hundred years by the Jewish faithful, such prayers had long been emptied of possible fulfillment and were seen as merely a poetic remembrance of things past. By the late nineteenth century many Western Jews were so identified with their countries of residence that any actual plan or program to create a real Jewish state was viewed as a direct threat to their own identities as loyal Germans, Frenchmen, Britishers, or Americans.

For Herzl and his followers Zionism was an attempt to end the eighteen hundred years of Jewish homelessness and dispersion throughout the world. It was an attempt to end the Jewish powerlessness that often resulted from being a pariah people, living in many nations but truly belonging nowhere. Zionism took its name from one of Jerusalem's historic hills, and it combined a deep biblical faith with an oppressed people's yearning for national freedom. With its very name, the Jewish national liberation movement linked itself to a real place in the real world, and it was Herzl's genius that welded the ancient longing with modern organizational skills and a concrete platform of action. Zionism sought to restore not only political independence to the Jewish people, but it also aimed to create a spiritual renaissance and a sense of self-esteem among the Jewish people who had endured eighteen centuries of persecution, hatred, expulsion, and genocide.

Yet by 1948, Zionism as a movement had not enrolled a majority of the world's Jews to its banner, and it faced the twin enemies of an unfriendly British mandate power and hostile Middle Eastern Arab leadership. It also faced a third and most tragic obstacle: the Nazi Holocaust. Fully one-third of the Jewish people, six million men, women, and children, were murdered by the Nazis and their collaborators between 1933 and 1945. The Holocaust had destroyed many of the European Jewish communities that had rallied to Herzl's dramatic message of hope and national independence, but the Nazis had also murdered those anti-Zionist Jews of Europe who had so resolutely proclaimed their allegiance to Germany, France, and other Western nations. It was one of the many bitter lessons of the Holocaust that the Jewish people in mandate Palestine and in the Diaspora would not forget.

The overwhelming horror of the Holocaust filled the Jews of Palestine with a sense of desperation that manifested itself in a bloody and exhausting war in 1948 and 1949, the Israeli war of independence. It was fought first against the British and then against the Arabs. The latter struggle has not yet ended except for the 1979 Egyptian-Israeli peace treaty.

The first years of British rule in Palestine, beginning in 1917, brought improved living and health standards to both Jews and Arabs, increased opportunities for education, and high hopes for an enlightened "Western" rule in a land that had suffered from four hundred years of a corrupt and inefficient Ottoman Turkish regime. The British conquest promised a new era of a just, humane, and competent government in Palestine.

Although Britain had suffered enormous human and financial losses in World War I, it still possessed a highly experienced colonial civil service as well as an effective police and military power. The Palestinians of the post–World War I period, both Jews and Arabs, confidently expected the bribes, the capricious execution of justice, and the official governmental neglect, all part of the Turkish rule, to end with the British mandate. Many Jews openly rejoiced that Turkey had been on the losing side in the war and that Britain had captured Jerusalem in December 1917 under the leadership of General Edmund Allenby.

The Jews of Palestine had another reason to welcome the British. In November 1917, the British government publicly issued a brief, official statement that would be known forever as the Balfour Declaration, named for the British foreign minister of the time, Arthur J. Balfour.

The British Cabinet, led by Prime Minister David Lloyd George, authorized Balfour to send the following letter to Lord Walter Rothschild, an English Zionist leader:

Dear Lord Rothschild:

I have much pleasure in conveying to you, on behalf of His Majesty's Government, the following declaration of sympathy with Jewish Zionist aspirations, which has been submitted to, and approved by, the cabinet.

"His Majesty's Government views with favour the establishment in Palestine of a national home for the Jewish people, and will use their best endeavours to facilitate the achievement of this object, it being clearly understood that nothing shall be done which might prejudice the civil and religious rights of existing non-Jewish communities in Palestine, or the rights and political status enjoyed by Jews in any other country."

Despite its carefully nuanced language and its cautious tone that left the future of Palestine wide open, the Balfour Declaration was greeted with elation and a sense of celebration by the downtrodden, war-weary Jewish masses. They neither knew nor cared about the complex struggle that preceded the publication of the Declaration. Nor did the deliberately vague phrase, "a national home for the Jewish people," deter them from their joy. The Balfour Declaration was the first official endorsement of Zionist aspirations by a major government in modern times.

For over sixty years scholars have tried to discover the British government's motivation and purpose in issuing the Declaration. In spite of their best efforts, however, we still know very little about the reasons for the British Cabinet's actions. The Balfour Declaration provided Great Britain with no political, military, or economic benefit. Perhaps the Declaration was, as Sir Mark Sykes, an official of the British foreign ministry of the time, put it, "the last wholly independent imperial act of a British government done without any reference at all to pressure from any other great state or combination of states." The Jewish masses in their instinctive understanding were, of course, correct. The Balfour Declaration, coming only twenty years after the Basel Zionist Congress, gave Zionism the international acceptance and attention that Herzl had sought. The small booklet, *Der Judenstaat*, and the single paragraph of the Balfour Declaration had propelled the Jewish people and their passion for the land of Israel onto the center stage of world history.

The years immediately after World War I also provided hope for possible Jewish-Arab cooperation and reconciliation in the Middle East. The modern Jewish and Arab nationalist movements first emerged in the late nineteenth and early twentieth centuries. From the outset they have been in direct confrontation and conflict over the answer to one critical and essential question: Who shall exercise national sovereignty and political control over the land called Israel by one group and Palestine by the other?

With the end of the Ottoman Turkish rule in 1917, both Jews and Arabs sensed the beginning of a new era, and for one brief moment genuine rapprochement seemed possible. The first Arab reaction to the Balfour Declaration was not totally negative. Surprisingly, two Arab leaders addressed a Zionist rally in London a month after the Decla-

ration was issued. Two leading Cairo newspapers were friendly, with
one asserting that the Arab people had nothing to fear from a Jewish
state since the British government had, in the Balfour Declaration,
simply recognized the historic Jewish rights in Palestine.

In 1918, Emir Faisal, who would later become king of Syria and
then of Iraq, met with Chaim Weizmann, a prominent Zionist leader
(thirty years later Weizmann would himself become Israel's first
president). Under the Ottoman Turks, Palestine had been a province
of Syria; hence Faisal's interest in the matter. Both Faisal and Weizmann blamed the Turks for creating discord between Arabs and
Jews, a charge that would soon be hurled at the British as well. With
the defeat of the Turks, a brighter chapter was at hand for the two
Semitic "cousins." A leading paper in Mecca, the very heart of the
Islamic religion, welcomed the Jews who were "coming home" to
Palestine: "the original sons of the country from which their Arab
brethren would benefit materially as well as spiritually."

In January 1919, Faisal and Weizmann signed a joint agreement
in which the Arab leader spoke of "the Arab state and Palestine." It
was clearly understood at the time that the latter, Palestine, was to
be a Jewish state with "the most cordial goodwill and understanding"
between the two states. The agreement also called for "all necessary
measures to encourage and stimulate immigration of Jews into Palestine on a large scale and as quickly as possible to settle Jewish immigrants upon the land." Two months later, in March 1919, Faisal
wrote to Felix Frankfurter, then an American Zionist leader and a
future United States Supreme Court justice:

> We are working together for a reformed and revived Near East, and
> our two movements complement one another. The Jewish movement
> is nationalist, not imperialist . . . and there is room in Syria [the
> Ottoman Turkish province that encompassed Palestine] for us both.
> We wish the Jews a most hearty welcome home.

Faisal added a quite reasonable provision to his agreement with
Weizmann. The Arab leader would abide by the agreement only if
an Arab state were established along with a Jewish one, and his demand was directed to the British government, the new ruling power
in the Middle East. In the years since World War I, not one but
several independent Arab states have been formally created out of

the old Ottoman empire: Lebanon, Syria, Iraq, Jordan, Yemen, and Saudi Arabia.

Unfortunately, a few months after his agreement with Weizmann and his letter to Frankfurter, Faisal backed away from both. In time, some Arabs charged that Faisal had been deceived by the two Jewish leaders and that the Arab ruler had also been misled by his interpreter, the famous T. E. Lawrence. Both charges seem implausible since the record of Faisal's meetings with the Zionist figures was quickly made public and, given Lawrence's well-known sympathy for the Arabs, it is most unlikely that he would mislead a leading Arab figure like Faisal in such important negotiations. Faisal later claimed that he did not even remember Frankfurter.

It would not be the last time that a moderate Arab leader beat a speedy retreat when faced with his own people's extreme positions. In fact, it would be nearly sixty years before another Arab leader, President Anwar el-Sadat of Egypt, publicly acknowledged the legitimacy of Jewish national rights and of the state of Israel itself. Sadat's assassination by extremists within the Egyptian army clearly demonstrates how difficult it has been for Arab leaders to move toward mutual recognition and peace with Israel.

The window of possible peace between Arabs and Jews that was opened so briefly with the defeat of the Turks in 1917 and with the Faisal-Weizmann agreement was quickly slammed shut and has only been partially reopened. The high hopes of 1917 to 1919 for a fair and sympathetic British mandate in Palestine were also dashed as London pursued the usual tactics of a colonial power: divide and conquer the subject peoples, make conflicting promises to both Jews and Arabs, attempt to repress or control the national leadership of both peoples, tolerate and even encourage tension and friction between Jews and Arabs, and finally, in the face of two seemingly irreconcilable forces and claims, abdicate responsibility and give up the mandate, leaving the two peoples to fight each other in a series of costly wars.

By 1948, the British government's policies and actions had become morally bankrupt and politically impotent. The British foreign minister of the time, Ernest Bevin, fiercely opposed the creation of a Jewish state. All in all, it was a wretched ending to the British mandate that had begun with such high hopes. The radical shift in only thirty years from Arthur Balfour's sympathy and understanding of Zionism to Ernest Bevin's bitter opposition is another reality of modern Israel.

Zionism, the movement that brought the state of Israel into being, is part of that reality as well. No other movement has attracted as much world attention or has evoked such intense emotion as Zionism. For its adherents, Zionism is the dynamic national liberation movement of the Jewish people. It has been the driving force and rallying cry in creating a Jewish state. As a national renaissance movement, it has helped restore self-esteem and a sense of inner strength to a badly battered people. Its goal of a just, free, secure, and compassionate Jewish state remains a guiding principle of Zionism today. In addition to a physical restoration of the Jewish people to their ancient homeland, Zionism has also called for a spiritual and cultural renewal of Judaism. Herzl declared in 1897 that "Zionism is the return to Judaism before the return to the Jewish land."

To its critics, Zionism is a distortion of Jewish ideals, a misreading of universal religious values. Zionism has created a parochial nation-state, Israel, that is based on a narrow political nationalism. Zionism and the emergence of the state of Israel have provided neither Jewish physical security nor an end to anti-Semitism, two fundamental goals of the entire Zionist endeavor.

To its enemies, Zionism is an aggressive nationalist movement that has forcibly expelled an indigenous people, the Palestinian Arabs, from their native land. In their place Zionism has established, at great human cost, an expansionist and militaristic state with a paranoid "we/they" view of history. In 1975, the United Nations General Assembly, which in 1947 had called for the creation of a Jewish state in Palestine, condemned Zionism as "racist" in its practices, despite the strenuous objections of the United States, Canada, and other nations.

All three groups—adherents, critics, and enemies—are passionate in their beliefs about Zionism; each one is ardently convinced that its own description is the authentic and correct one. But what are the origins and foundations of this hotly debated movement?

The link between the Jewish people and the land of Israel began thousands of years ago during the biblical period. The land was regarded as an eternal, irrevocable gift from God to his people, part of an everlasting covenant:

> Therefore shall ye keep all the commandments which I command you this day, that ye may be strong, and go in and possess the land . . . and that ye may prolong your days upon the land which the Lord swore to your fathers to give unto them and to their seed, a land flowing with milk and honey . . . a land which the Lord thy God careth for; the eyes of the Lord thy God are always upon it, from the beginning of the year unto the end of the year (Deut. 11:8, 9,12, KJV).

God is, of course, the ultimate owner of the land and, indeed, the owner of all the lands of the world. But the Jewish people then, now, and always are the earthly inheritors of the land of Israel, God's permanent tenants.

This theological belief was first articulated in the Hebrew Bible and then amplified and reemphasized in the Jewish postbiblical writings of the Midrash and the Talmud.* The liturgy of the synagogue and home also developed this deeply felt faith commitment. The annual cycle of Jewish religious holidays was based on the changing seasons in the land of Israel, and synagogues were built throughout the world so that the worshipper always faced toward Jerusalem.

In home observances of the Sabbath and Jewish holidays, when a Jew recited the prayers over food or at wedding ceremonies, or when a new house was built, or when words of solace and comfort were spoken to mourners—in all these moments of both community and personal life, the hope for a national restoration to the land of Israel was always present:

> Blessed be Thou who is building Jerusalem (grace after meals).

> May the Lord comfort you among all those that mourn for Zion and Jerusalem (prayer said to mourners).

---

*Midrash ("inquiry")—a vast body of literature that interprets the Hebrew Bible (the "Written Law") in nonlegal, nonliteral terms. The Midrash generally employs hermeneutical laws of interpretation. *Talmud* ("teaching")—the comprehensive written record of Judaism's "Oral Law" containing the numerous discussions, comments, and authoritative laws derived from the Bible. The Talmud is the result of eight centuries of study in Babylonia and the land of Israel.

May Zion rejoice as her children are restored to her in joy. O Lord our God, may there soon be heard in the cities of Judah and in the streets of Jerusalem, the voice of joy and gladness, the voice of bride and groom . . . the voice of young people feasting and singing (Jewish wedding liturgy).

Remember Mount Zion, remember O Lord, the affection of Jerusalem, never forget the love of Zion; Thou wilt rise and have pity on Zion; for it is time to favor her, for the appointed time has come (penitential liturgy).

Have mercy O Lord, and return to Jerusalem, thy city . . . Bring us to Zion, thy city, with song to Jerusalem the site of thy sanctuary, with everlasting joy . . . (daily and festival liturgy).

Sound the ram's horn to herald our freedom. Raise high the banner to gather our exiles. Gather our dispersed from the four corners of the earth. Praised are you O Lord, who gathers our exiles (daily afternoon service).

Next year in Jerusalem! (conclusion of Passover Seder service).

The geography of the land of Israel was studied in great detail by Jews throughout the Diaspora. The names and locations of Israel's mountains, deserts, valleys, rivers, seas, and cities became part of the Jew's basic education. The very names—Mount Zion, Mount Carmel, the River Jordan, the Sea of Galilee, Jerusalem, Tiberias, Hebron, Jaffa—all echoed and resonated in countless schoolhouses, synagogues, and homes during the eighteen hundred years of Jewish homelessness. Songs and prayers extolling the land were chanted in the thousands of towns and villages of the Diaspora on every continent of the globe. The land of Israel remained the focus of Jewish yearning, affection, and love. For seventy generations after the Roman destruction of Jerusalem in A.D. 70, Jews gave voice to their passion for the land and to their profound and unshakable faith in their national restoration. The belief that the Jewish people would someday return to their homeland became a vital component of religious law, liturgy, and tradition.

This eternal love for Eretz Israel was, however, always concrete, real, and earthly. The Mishnah* asserts that the "land of Israel is

---

Mishnah ("repeated teaching")—the first part of the Talmud.

holier than all other lands" because it is only there that certain rituals can be performed. The Talmud rules that "in the case of one who purchases a house in the land of Israel, the deed may be written even on the Sabbath." And in one place in the Talmud, a rabbi goes so far as to say, "Whoever lives outside the land of Israel can be regarded as an idolater." The Jewish passion for the land is rooted in a flesh-and-blood, real-time place—a land filled with prayers, joys, sorrows, seedtimes and harvests, droughts and floods, life and death.

That inextricable bond with the land began with the Hebrew patriarchs and matriarchs: Abraham, Isaac, Jacob, Sarah, Rebecca, Leah, and Rachel. The biblical Book of Genesis graphically recounts their lives and sojournings in the land then called Canaan. According to Jewish tradition, Rachel, Jacob's second wife and the mother of Joseph, is buried in Bethlehem, while the other six fathers and mothers of the Jewish people are buried in the Cave of Machpelah in Hebron. Genesis ends with the death of Joseph in Egypt, but he promises his people that God will "bring them up to the land He swore to Abraham, Isaac, and Jacob."

The stirring theme of the Exodus from Egypt has been a source of hope and inspiration to oppressed men and women throughout history. What is sometimes overlooked, however, in the extraordinary emphasis given to Moses and his confrontation with the Pharaoh, is the ultimate objective of the Exodus. The objective was not merely to escape from slavery and to seek freedom, but physically to bring the descendants of the patriarchs and matriarchs back to the land that God had promised them. So powerful was the people's link with the land of Canaan, even at that early moment in Jewish history, that the Hebrew slaves brought Joseph's casket with them when they left Egypt. Joseph, the great-grandson of Abraham, was not to be permanently buried in the strange land of Egypt but rather in the land promised to his people by God. The Exodus event was the first instance of a Diaspora community "coming home."

Moses insisted that his ragtag group of former slaves was not sufficiently strong, physically or spiritually, for the rigors of freedom in the land of Canaan. Forty years in the wilderness had to pass until a new generation, one born in freedom, could enter the Promised Land. Even Moses himself could not enter the Land, and he, too, died outside of it. The successful entry and conquest was left to his young disciple, Joshua. Scholars place the Exodus at about 1230 B.C.

After Joshua came the turbulent period of the Judges, which continued until the first independent Jewish commonwealth began with King David about 980 B.C. David made Jerusalem his royal capital, and it was there that Solomon, David's son, built the Holy Temple. The first commonwealth lasted until the Babylonians, led by King Nebuchadnezzar, destroyed Jerusalem in 586 B.C.

The conquerors demolished the Temple and sent the survivors to Babylon as captives, the first of several such traumatic events in Jewish history. But only forty years later, Cyrus, a Persian king, captured Babylonia and allowed the Jewish exiles to return to Jerusalem. About forty thousand did go back, and in 515 B.C. the Second Temple was completed. During this period, two important leaders emerged in Jerusalem. The first, Ezra, spiritually revived and reeducated the exiles to the laws of God and the Torah, while Nehemiah supervised the physical reconstruction of Jerusalem, the Holy City. It was a leadership model that was to be followed in other periods of history, but most especially during the last one hundred years. Zionism has meant both the spiritual and the physical restoration of the Jewish people; one kind of renewal without the other is incomplete and inadequate.

But the Babylonian experience was also a model in other ways. First, a foreign power invaded and conquered the land of Israel. Most of the Jews were either killed or exiled by the new ruling power; the few who remained were not allowed to live in Jerusalem or even in the land itself. Despite these cruel edicts, a small and faithful Jewish community remained in the land as a "saving remnant," waiting until larger numbers of their brothers and sisters returned to the land and revivified the *Yishuv* (the Jewish community in the land of Israel). This pattern of destruction, dispersion, saving remnant, return, and rebirth has been repeated several times during the long span of Jewish history as, for example, in the sixth century B.C. and, more recently, in the nineteenth and twentieth centuries.

Although Cyrus granted permission for the exiled Jews to return to Zion and the land of Israel, some chose to remain in their new homes in Babylon. The Diaspora, too, has therefore been a continuing feature of Jewish life. The national center in the land of Israel has sometimes been large in size, as in our own day; sometimes it has been small in number, depending on who had political sovereignty and control over the land. But there was always a series of Jewish communities outside the land of Israel. The Diaspora, or dispersion, was sometimes large and sometimes small in number, depending on the various political, social, religious, and economic forces that were at work in history. The land of Israel and its Jewish community is the center of the "Jewish wheel," while the Diaspora communities constitute the spokes and the rim of the wheel.

Following the period of Ezra and Nehemiah, the Yishuv lived under a number of foreign rulers, including the Persians, the Greeks of Alexander the Great, and the Seleucids (a Greco-Syrian regime that controlled the land of Israel after Alexander's death in 323 B.C.). One of the Seleucid kings, Antiochus, attempted to impose a monolithic and alien religion over the Jews of Israel. Antiochus banned the study of the Torah and the observance of Jewish rituals and liturgy. In effect, this was an assault on the very existence of Judaism. A revolt broke out, and a small band of Jews led by Judas Maccabeus conducted a victorious three-year guerrilla-warfare campaign against Antiochus's large standing army. In 165 B.C., Judas reclaimed the Holy Temple in Jerusalem and rededicated it to the service of Israel's God. This brilliant victory (Judas Maccabeus is today a member of West Point's military "Hall of Fame") is commemorated each year with the celebration of the festival of Hanukkah, or Dedication.

Judas and the Jewish rulers who came after him exercised political sovereignty in the land of Israel until the Romans, yet another foreign ruler, arrived in Jerusalem in 63 B.C. Relations between the Jews and the Romans, the occupied and the occupiers in the land of Israel, were always tense and uneasy at best, and bloody and murderous at worst. There were four wars of Jewish rebellion against the Romans within a hundred years. These brutal wars resulted in the destruction of the Temple in A.D. 70 (ending the second independent Jewish commonwealth), the mass suicides of nearly one thousand Jewish zealots on Massada in A.D. 73, and a final crushing defeat at the hands of the Romans in A.D. 135.

Historians estimate that five hundred eighty thousand Jews were killed in these wars out of a total Jewish population of five million! Nine hundred eighty-five cities, towns, and villages were destroyed, including the capital city of Jerusalem. Many Jews were taken prisoner and brought in chains to Rome. Titus, one of the victorious Roman generals, erected a memorial arch in his honor to celebrate his conquest of Judea, the Roman name for the land of Israel. One of the sculptured bas-reliefs on the arch in Rome is a group of vanquished Jewish prisoners carrying the Holy Temple's sacred seven-branched candelabrum, the menorah, into captivity.

The futile wars against imperial Rome were a national catastrophe for the Jewish nation. The Temple was destroyed, and the Holy City was razed to the ground. Jews were expelled from their land, the countryside was devastated, and the Romans built a new city over the ruins of Jerusalem, naming it Aelia Capitolina. No Jew was allowed to enter this new city, which was dedicated to the god Jupiter. The Romans also renamed the entire country. No more was it to be called Judea; the new name was Syria Palestina in honor of the Philistines, the ancient enemies of Samson, King Saul, and King David.

The holy covenant between God and the Jewish people seemed ended and the link with the land of Israel shattered. The Romans minted victory coins after the last Jewish war in 135 carrying the two words: *Judea capta,* that is, "Judea is defeated." Like other ancient peoples who had lost both their land and their political independence, the Jews appeared ripe for extinction, ready to disappear from the stage of history forever. But Judea did not die, neither its people nor their passion for the land.

For eighteen hundred years the Jews kept alive the belief in a return to the homeland. Small centers of piety and scholarship grew up in the Diaspora, and an inverse ratio began to work among the Jewish communities outside the land of Israel. As living conditions became worse, as the political and religious persecutions increased, the Jewish belief in the eventual return to Zion became even greater. Each year the Jews sadly remembered the loss of their land, and each year they reaffirmed their faith that the biblical "land of milk and honey," the land of Jewish shepherds, vineyard keepers, and farmers, would again be restored.

The immense power and stubborn persistence of this deeply felt faith cannot be overemphasized. Without that faith the national identity of the Jewish people and, perhaps, their actual existence might have ended. The relentless record of persecution, expulsion, forced religious conversion, and, finally, genocide nearly destroyed all Jewish life on earth, but the hope for a return to the land of Israel helped the Jews endure all their sufferings.

Judah ha-Levi (A.D. 1086–1141), a physician and Hebrew poet, expressed that hope in his magnificent "Odes to Zion." Even today these remain unequaled in their exquisite and powerful evocation of his love for the land. Born in Spain, ha-Levi sought to reach Zion but was unsuccessful in his pilgrimage. He died in Egypt, where he is also buried:

> My heart is in the East, and I am in the farthest
> West . . . I am the harp for all thy [Zion] songs . . .
> Would that I had wings that I could wend my way
>   to Thee, O Jerusalem, from afar!
> I will make my own broken heart find its way
>   amidst your broken ruins;
> I will fall upon my face to the ground for I
>   take much delight in your stones and
>   show favor in your very dust.
> The air of your land is the very life of our soul.

The unbroken record of eighteen hundred years of faithfulness to a Zion reborn is one more reality of modern Israel. But there is another reality that is virtually unknown to many people, including Jews. It is the fact that there were always Jewish communities, a Jewish presence in the land of Israel during those eighteen centuries stretching from the Roman conquest to the rebirth of a Jewish state. A widely held misconception is that *all* of the Jews were expelled from the land, that the land was empty of Jews, and that only in the nineteenth century did they begin to return. The truth is much different.

The late James Parkes, a distinguished English Christian scholar, wrote: "The real title deeds [of the Jewish people] were written by the . . . heroic endurance of those who had maintained a Jewish presence in the land through the centuries, and in spite of every discouragement." It is beyond the scope of this work to describe in detail the truth of Parkes's statement, but a few examples will help illustrate the permanent "Jewish presence in the land."

Perhaps the most dramatic example is the small village of Peki'in in northern Galilee which has had a continuous Jewish community since the days of the Second Temple. The Jews of Peki'in were never exiled from the land of Israel, and for twenty-five hundred years they have tilled their land and bred their silkworms. The ancient Peki'in synagogue, restored over a hundred years ago, was first built in the second century A.D. with stones that were brought from Jerusalem after the destruction of the Temple.

With the end of armed Jewish resistance to Rome in A.D. 135, the few surviving Jews moved north to Galilee and began a quiet period of farming, study, and prayer. The Mishnah was completed there, and the Palestinian Talmud was composed there as well. But in A.D. 313, the Jews of the land faced a new challenge. Emperor Constantine, who controlled Syria Palestina, formally adopted Christianity and made it the official state religion. Christian theology of the period already reflected an animus to both the idea and the possible reality of a reborn Jewish state. Jews, it was believed, had denied the divinity of Jesus three centuries earlier and were condemned by God to be scattered and punished for their sin of not accepting the Messiah who had dwelt among them. The Byzantine Christian rulers in the three hundred years following Constantine severely repressed the Yishuv, which still somehow managed to number forty-three communities in the land.

In A.D. 632, a new and important group, the Arab Muslims, captured Palestine from the Christians, holding it for over four hundred fifty years. Interestingly, not once during those four and one-half centuries did the Arabs make Jerusalem their capital. Instead, in A.D. 716 they established a new city, Ramla, as a seat of governing power. Ramla, which is near modern Israel's international airport, is the only city which the Arabs founded in Palestine during their long rule. Real Arab political power came from either Damascus, Baghdad, or Cairo, all outside the land of Israel.

The Yishuv's relationship with the Arab Muslims in those years was ambivalent and complex. Sometimes the rulers carried out bloody actions against the Jews of the land, sometimes the Arabs practiced a kind of benign neglect, and sometimes there was a mild toleration of Palestinian Jewry. By the eleventh century the number of Jewish communities had grown to fifty.

In the summer of 1099, a thousand years after the Roman destruction of Jerusalem, another European group conquered Jerusalem. This time it was the Christian Crusaders under the leadership of the duke of Lower Lorraine, Godfrey of Bouillon. During the siege of the city, Jews and Arabs fought together against the common enemy —the knights from Western Europe. Godfrey and his forces massacred the surviving Jews and Muslims, often burning them alive, and the Crusaders forbade all non-Christians from even setting foot in the Holy City. The Crusaders' rule was a short one, lasting only eighty-eight years, and their human legacy was one of carnage and murder of the "infidels." Their architectural legacy, however, consists of a number of remarkable churches and castles that still dot the Israeli countryside and are today tourist attractions.

After the Crusaders came the Mamelukes, the Ottoman Turks, and finally, the British. The seemingly endless number of foreign rulers in the land is another reality of Israel.

From this bewildering mélange of place names, battle dates, noble and ignoble warriors, religious fanatics, emperors, caliphs, sultans, knights, bishops, kings, queens, popes, imams, and prime ministers, the stunning reality of Jewish continuity in the land of Israel clearly emerges. Often caught between the twin pincers of the Christian cross and the Islamic crescent, the Jews of the Yishuv managed to survive as dyers and tanners, philosophers, rabbis, religious mystics, farmers, glassblowers, traders in grain and spices, and producers of olives, cotton, barley, silkworms and wine. Amazingly, they somehow clung to their land, never surrendering their title deeds to the many foreign rulers who, with their armies, came and departed with such painful regularity.

In the midst of armed invasions, religious hatreds, and human butchery, the Jews of the land still managed to be fathers and mothers who transmitted their belief in Zion's restoration from one generation to the next. We know very few of their names, but these men and women kept the flickering flame of Jewish national hope alive for eighteen hundred years.

The Yishuv produced a great work of religious mysticism, the *Cabala*, and the Jews of the land of Israel also wrote definitive legal texts that are still studied and followed today. In 1577, one of the first Hebrew printing presses was set up in the Galilean city of Safad. The continued Jewish presence in Palestine for eighteen hundred years had a transcendent purpose: to cling tenaciously to the land of Israel in preparation for the expected and yearned-for restoration of an independent Jewish commonwealth. It was as if the Jewish people had been forcibly removed from their sanctuary, but a faithful few kept the holy vessels and objects polished and ready for the time when the congregation of Israel would return to its sanctuary and reclaim its homeland.

In the fifteenth century, four hundred years before the modern Zionist movement began, a Christian visitor to the land of Israel observed:

> The heathen oppress them at their pleasure. They know that the Jews think and say this is the Holy Land that was promised to them. Those of them who live here are regarded as holy by the other Jews, for in spite of all the tribulations and the agonies they suffer at the hands of the heathen, *they refuse to leave the place* [emphasis added].

When they were able, the Jewish communities in the Diaspora sent money to the Yishuv. These contributions were used to support schools, synagogues, and other communal institutions. Some elderly Jews came to the land to die and be buried in the sacred soil, while others came, when the Turkish authorities permitted it, to study and to pray. By the year 1800, however, the number of Jews in Palestine had fallen to between ten and fifteen thousand. As the Ottoman Turkish Empire entered the last century of its existence, Palestine became more and more a backward province, an area in decline. Its cities were poverty stricken, its fields and orchards increasingly barren, and its countryside a wasteland.

Mark Twain visited Palestine in 1867 and wrote:

> Desolate country whose soil is rich enough, but is given over wholly to weeds. . . . We reached Tabor safely. . . . We never saw a human being on the whole route. . . . There was hardly a tree or shrub anywhere. Even the olive and the cactus . . . had almost deserted the country. . . . Palestine sits in sackcloth and ashes.

As the nineteenth century came to a close, the Ottoman Turkish persecution of the Jews continued amidst a shrinking economic base in Palestine. The Yishuv, a once proud community, was becoming more and more dependent on financial contributions from the Diaspora. The strength of the Palestinian Jewish community was ebbing away.

Was national restoration and rebirth only a myth, a pious hope, a cruel hoax? Were the eighteen long and bitter centuries all in vain? Were the grim realities of Jewish life too overwhelming even for the faithful saving remnant? Was the Prophet Jeremiah's description of Jerusalem, written so long ago, to be the final word?

> How doth the city sit solitary,
> That was full of people!
> How is she become as a widow!
> She that was great among the nations,
> And princess among the provinces,
> How is she become tributary!
> —Lam. 1:1, *KJV*

In such critical and desperate situations in the lives of individuals and nations, one of two things usually happens: either there is a complete breakdown of body and spirit with illness and death soon following, or there is a complete breakthrough of body and spirit leading to health and renewed life. Breakdown or breakthrough? For the Jewish people the answer was not long in coming.

2 | *The Rise of Modern Zionism*

Sometimes a single traumatic event can radically change all previous actions and patterns of behavior. Such an event may temporarily stun a person or group into passivity and inaction. But it can also be a life-changing experience leading to new and daring actions whose results can never be accurately predicted.

Two such momentous events were the anti-Jewish pogroms in czarist Russia in 1881, and the Dreyfus trial in France in 1893. The first event profoundly affected the entire Jewish people, while the second decisively changed the life of an individual Jew. Both events were transforming in their power, and ultimately they altered the course of Jewish and world history.

In 1881, half of the world's Jews, some five million people, lived in czarist Russia. Many Russian Jews, while remaining faithful to the traditional religious values including the hope for a restored Zion, also believed that their political emancipation was near. After centuries of czarist tyranny, severe anti-Jewish legislation, and repeated acts of violent persecution, it was widely felt that Russia, especially under the progressive leadership of Czar Alexander II, would soon become a constitutional monarchy following the enlightened models of France and Great Britain. The granting of full citizenship and civil rights appeared imminent for Russia's Jews.

But in 1881, Alexander II was assassinated by reactionary elements within Russia. His murder was followed by a wave of pogroms directed at Jews throughout the country. The pogroms were officially sanctioned physical attacks that were organized and condoned by the new repressive regime of Czar Alexander III. Previously many Jews had naively believed that Russian anti-Semitism was felt only by the poor and illiterate peasants of the country, and not by the educated leaders and rulers. But after the terrifying and murderous pogroms of 1881 and the passage of new and even more cruel anti-Jewish legislation, the infamous "May Laws" of 1882, it became absolutely clear that czarist Russia was the implacable foe of the Jewish people.

Beginning in 1881, millions of Jews left Russia for the United States and other lands of freedom. Some Russian Jews remained and became anticzarist revolutionaries, joining the many Marxist and socialist underground political parties of the day. Still others sought to make the eighteen-hundred-year-old hope of Jewish national restoration a reality. By 1881, yearning and longing for Zion was no longer enough in the face of a violent anti-Semitic czarist regime that killed and persecuted Jewish men, women, and children as part of its official policy. What was needed was a program of action to save the Jewish people from a pogrom-filled existence.

Thousands of idealistic young Russian Jews organized themselves into a political and cultural group called the "Lovers of Zion." They were unable to hold a convention inside Russia because the czarist authorities deemed the group dangerous. Instead, the "Lovers of Zion" met in Constantinople. The year was 1882.

The young Zionists issued a manifesto to "our brothers and sisters in Exile." "What have you been doing until 1882? Sleeping and dreaming the false dream of assimilation [and emancipation]. . . . The star of your future is gleaming in the East [the land of Israel]. . . . We want a home in our country. It was given to us by the mercy of God; it is ours as registered in the archives of history. . . . [We will] beg it of the Sultan himself, and if it is impossible to obtain this, beg that we may at least possess it as a state within a larger state. . . ."

The 1882 manifesto was a significant step in the growth of modern Zionism for two reasons. First, it called upon Jews everywhere to join and support a "society" whose goal was to obtain "a home in our country." Second, the young "Lovers of Zion" urged political action in the real world. The quaint nineteenth century use of the verb "beg" should not obscure the important fact that the manifesto demanded an end to eighteen hundred years of faithful, but passive, waiting.

It is interesting that the authors of this early Zionist platform were prepared to settle for something less than total national Jewish independence. That specific demand would come some years later. The violent anti-Semitism of the Russian authorities in 1881 and 1882 had energized a large number of Jews to take action at last. The hope for a restored Zion had now moved forever from the intimacy and privacy of the synagogue and the Jewish home. Zionism as a national movement had entered the outside world.

A single event that took place in Paris nearly fifteen years later transformed a journalist and playwright into a national leader and a world figure. Theodor Herzl (1860–1904), a sophisticated and thoroughly assimilated Austrian Jew, was chief Paris correspondent for a leading Viennese newspaper in the early 1890s. Like other progressive thinkers of his time, Herzl deeply admired France and her revolutionary ideals of *liberté, égalité, fraternité.*

France was the lodestar for liberal thought and political enlightenment in Europe. So the arrest, trial, public disgrace, and imprisonment of a French Jewish army officer, Alfred Dreyfus, during the 1890s, shattered the young reporter who covered what came to be known as "L'affaire Dreyfus." Captain Dreyfus was falsely accused of having sold French military secrets to Germany. Anti-Semitism was a key factor when high-ranking French army officers knowingly made Dreyfus the innocent scapegoat for someone else's crime. After Dreyfus, a hapless victim, was found guilty of treason by an army court-martial, he was stripped of his rank in a degrading public ceremony that Herzl and many others witnessed in Paris. Herzl was utterly depressed when the French crowd shouted, "A bas les juifs!" ("Death to the Jews!") as Dreyfus was being humiliated. The Viennese journalist noted in his diary that the hostile crowd did not shout "Death to the traitor!" or even "Death to Dreyfus!" Rather, it was the chilling and classic anti-Semitic cry of "Death to the Jews!"

Herzl personally identified with Dreyfus who was, like himself, highly acculturated and removed from his Jewish origins. Herzl sadly concluded that anti-Semitism, or hatred of the Jews, was a permanent part of European society, even in enlightened and progressive France. Even when Jews like Dreyfus and Herzl attempted to assimilate into the larger society, it was to no avail. Anti-Semitism persisted. Herzl became disillusioned with the "clamor against the Jews" and, in a prophetic sense, understood that there was no future for the Jewish people in Europe: "We shall not be left in peace."

Herzl's answer to this painful conclusion was a personal break-through for him: "the restoration of the Jewish state." "Am I ahead of my time? Are the sufferings of the Jews not yet acute enough? We shall see." Almost as an act of self-discovery, Herzl declared: "We are a people—one people." The assimilated prodigal son had come home to his people bringing with him a powerful call: "The world needs a Jewish state, therefore, it will arise." It was needed, Herzl believed, to end anti-Semitism with all its oppression and persecution.

Herzl followed his pessimistic analysis with a daring idea: the mass emigration of Jews from their countries of residence. "It will be a re-lief from the old burden [anti-Semitism] which all [Jews and Christians] have suffered." He was convinced the actual physical departure of the Jews from their various countries of residence would benefit everyone, including the host countries who did not want their Jews.

"No human being is wealthy or powerful enough to transfer an entire people from one place of residence to another. Only an idea can achieve that. The state idea surely has that power," Herzl wrote. Herzl outlined his bold plan for the Jewish state in great detail. Some of his specific ideas today seem bizarre, such as establishing dueling societies in the Jewish state. Herzl was, after all, a product of the Austrian society of his time which considered dueling an ennobling activity, a test of manhood.

Shaken by the Dreyfus affair, saddened by the persistence of anti-Semitism, obsessed with solving the "Jewish question," and "intoxi-cated" by his "gigantic dream" of a restored Jewish state, Herzl emptied his tormented soul into print and published a slim volume in 1896 with a dramatic title, *Der Judenstaat* (*The Jewish State*). That small pamphlet catapulted Zionism and the Jewish people into the world arena of *Realpolitik* and Herzl into immortality. *Der Judenstaat*, which has since been translated into nearly twenty lan-guages, made an instant impact upon Jews everywhere. It sparked sharp divisions within the Jewish community, and evoked intense emotion.

Incredibly, Herzl did not know of the 1882 manifesto, of the earlier Zionist thinkers of the nineteenth century, or of the "Lovers of Zion" societies that had been organized in Russia and other parts of Eastern Europe. Nor did he know a great deal about the rich Jewish religious tradition that focused so intensely on Zion and the land of Israel. Herzl was a genius, but not because he correctly diagnosed the problem of anti-Semitism. Others before him had done as well or better. Herzl's genius was that he majestically moved an entire people toward a noble and magnificent goal: "We shall live at last as free men on our soil, and in our own homes peacefully die."

The first Zionist Congress of 1897 was convened by Herzl, and it adopted the following statement of purpose: "Zionism seeks to secure for the Jewish people a publicly recognized, legally secured home in Palestine." Herzl was to attend only five other Congresses before he died, but he was able to establish the basic institutions and forms of the Zionist movement that have remained to our own day.

In the eight years following the publication of *Der Judenstaat*, Herzl carried out an exhausting schedule of Zionist activities and several bold but unsuccessful diplomatic attempts to obtain a Jewish state. He rushed from one meeting to another, from kaiser to sultan to pope to king to prime minister, and from country to country (he visited Palestine only once). His health and personal family life deteriorated and, in 1904 at the age of forty-four, he died of a heart attack. Both during and after his life he was revered, especially by the Jews of Eastern Europe.

There have been other outstanding Zionist and/or Israeli leaders since Herzl, but none of them has ever attained the "light mist of legend" (Herzl's own words) that has enveloped the charismatic founder of political Zionism and the chief architect of the state of Israel. Herzl's principles were called "political Zionism" because they were based primarily on diplomatic and political efforts. Perhaps because of his own limited Jewish education, Herzl did not emphasize what has been termed "spiritual Zionism," which made the ethical ideals of Judaism a necessary prerequisite for a physical restoration in the land of Israel. Critics of Herzlian Zionism were fearful that it might result in a Jewish state without Judaism, without Jewish values.

The leader of spiritual Zionism was Asher Ginzberg (1856–1927), who wrote in Hebrew under the pen name of Ahad Ha'am ("One of the People"). Born in the Ukraine and given a superior religious education, Ginzberg taught himself Russian, English, and other languages. He became a Zionist early in life and attended the first Zionist Congress in 1897, but never attended another. He held no office in the movement. His influence on Zionist thinking was achieved through his many essays, all written in flawless Hebrew.

Ahad Ha'am sought a gradual and systematic increase of the Jewish population in Palestine. More important to him than numbers, however, were Jewish cultural and spiritual values. Although he was an agnostic, he placed great stress upon many Jewish religious ideals. Ahad Ha'am taught that Zionism had to be concerned with authentic Jewish learning, culture, and history. It had to be both humanistic and humane in its actions and policies. The Zionist ideal was to be based on quality, not quantity. Ha'am did not believe that the "ingathering of the Exiles" could ever be achieved by any "national means," but only by "miraculous religion." Thus, he urged the "settlement of a small part of our people in Palestine," people who were spiritually prepared to return to the Jewish homeland. He feared that the future leaders of a Jewish state (he died twenty-one years before Israeli independence) would be "spiritually far removed from Judaism."

Nor did he have any illusions about the Jewish state itself:

> After two thousand years of untold misery and suffering, the Jewish people can not possibly be content with attaining at last to the position of a small and insignificant nation, with a state tossed about like a ball between its powerful neighbors, and maintaining its existence only by diplomatic shifts and continual trucking to the favored of fortune.

Ahad Ha'am was intensely proud of the "spirit of our people . . . which has prevented us from following the rest of the world along the beaten path." When he moved to Tel Aviv toward the end of his life, he attracted a group of disciples who made his brand of spiritual Zionism their own. Ahad Ha'am fervently believed that the fundamental principle of the future Jewish state "will be neither the ascendency of the body over the spirit, nor the suppression of the body for the spirit's sake, but the uplifting of the body by the spirit."

Six years after Ahad Ha'am died, Hitler became chancellor of Germany. Hitler's anti-Jewish policies, culminating in the Holocaust, overwhelmed Ahad Ha'am's position that the land of Israel is primarily a spiritual center of Jewish life. Millions of Jewish bodies as well as souls were destroyed between 1933 and 1945, and Jews throughout the world could not, therefore, overly worry about spiritual and moral values. Instead, the overriding concern was to save Jewish lives during the Holocaust and to bring Jews to Eretz Israel. The dialogue that Ahad Ha'am had begun, however, was suspended only temporarily. Today his arguments are heard again, though in an updated form, as Israelis debate what kind of nation and society they seek to create.

Several other schools of pre-1948 Zionist thought have also shaped contemporary Israeli values. One such school was led by the world famous philosopher, Martin Buber (1878–1965), who emigrated to Palestine from Germany in 1938 after the rise of Nazism. He became a distinguished faculty member at the Hebrew University in Jerusalem which, founded in 1925, chose an American reform rabbi from San Francisco, Judah Magnes (1877–1948), as its first president. Magnes and Buber were intellectual leaders of the binational movement within Zionism.

The two men were controversial during their lifetimes because they advocated a cooperative Jewish-Arab state with shared rights, shared responsibilities, and shared sovereignty. Both professors were deeply committed to the Jewish claim to the land of Israel. For Buber "something even higher than the life of our people is bound up in the land, namely, its work, its divine mission."

In 1929 the Arabs led a series of bloody riots against the Jews of Palestine. Despite the resulting anger and fear of his fellow Jews, Magnes in 1930 urged the Yishuv to "make every possible effort politically as well as in other ways to work hand in hand as teachers, helpers, friends—with the awakening Arab world . . . [using] all the weapons of civilization except bayonets: spiritual, intellectual, social, cultural, financial, economic, medical. . . ."

For Magnes, Palestine was "required for the fullest development of the Jewish people," but the Hebrew University president was prepared to "yield the Jewish state and the Jewish majority" in the land as long as his three primary Zionist goals were fulfilled in a binational "democratic regime": open Jewish immigration into the land, settlement on the land, and "Hebrew life and culture."

Buber's goal was a "Hebrew humanism" rather than "Jewish nationalism." He feared that the latter ideology was separate from Judaism, and his brand of Zionism was an organic fusion of both nationalism and religion, not unlike Ahad Ha'am's ideas. But Buber went further. In an extraordinarily strong letter written in 1939 to the Indian national leader, Mahatma Gandhi, Buber totally rejected Gandhi's "simple" claim that "Palestine belongs to the Arabs." Buber believed there were "two vital claims" to the land and that the goal of Zionism was "to reconcile both claims." "It must be possible to find some compromise. . . . We [Jews] love the land . . . such love and such faith are surely present on the other side as well. . . . Our settlers do not come here as colonists from the Occident to have natives do their work for them. . . . They themselves [the Jews] spend their strength and their blood to make the land fruitful. . . . We have no desire to dispossess [the Arabs]; we want to live with them."

During the 1930s and 1940s, Buber, Magnes, and other Jewish leaders who were committed to a binational state ardently searched for Arab counterparts who were also committed to Arab-Jewish cooperation. Formal and informal meetings were held with various Arabs, many of whom were unfortunately assassinated by Arab terrorists when it was discovered they were meeting with the Jewish "enemy" to discuss the possibility of a binational state that would recognize Jewish as well as Arab claims and rights.

In time the murders of Arab moderates by extremists destroyed any chances of a meaningful Arab-Jewish dialogue. By 1941, Magnes sadly concluded there was "no possibility of reaching an agreement with any responsible Arab on any other basis, for the next ten or fifteen years, except on the basis of a [Jewish] minority in this country." In effect, this meant the limiting of Jewish immigration into Palestine at a time when European Jewry faced physical annihilation. Any attempt to place a quota on Jewish immigration was completely unacceptable for every Jew, including Buber and Magnes.

The lofty goals of binationalism failed for psychological and historical reasons. A dialogue, as Buber so eloquently taught in his writings, demands two partners. But the Jewish binationalists were unable to find Arab partners who could enter into such a dialogue and survive the deadly terrorism of their own people. The use of political assassination within the Arab world remains a problem to this day.

The socialist wing of Zionism has played the dominant role in developing the ideology of the movement, and it profoundly shaped daily Jewish life in pre-1948 Palestine and in the state of Israel as well. Since so many of the early Zionist leaders came from the Eastern Europe of the late nineteenth and early twentieth centuries, it was only natural that they were deeply influenced by the emergence of socialism, a potent political force in that area of the world.

"Socialist Zionism" had many thinkers and leaders, but none was more important or beloved than Aaron David Gordon (1856–1922). Born and educated in the dynamic Russian Jewish community of his time, Gordon became a "Lover of Zion" at an early age. However, it was not until he was forty-seven and a husband and father that he left his white-collar job in Russia and emigrated to the land of Israel. There he preached and practiced the "religion of labor" among his fellow Jews.

For nearly twenty years, Gordon threw himself into arduous and exhausting physical labor. He worked in the vineyards, swamps, and fields, and all the while he taught that the Jew can find spiritual and national redemption only through *avodah*, the Hebrew term for labor and the worship of God. Jewish self-liberation comes with continuous contact with the soil of the Promised Land.

"The Jewish people have been completely cut off from nature and imprisoned within city walls these two thousand years. We have become accustomed to every form of life except to a life of labor . . . labor for its own sake," Gordon wrote. "We come to our homeland in order to be planted in our national soil from which we have been uprooted, to strike our roots deep into the life-giving substances and to stretch out in . . . the sunlight of the homeland. . . . What we seek to establish in Palestine is a new, recreated Jewish people."

Gordon lived out his Zionist commitment as a laborer, and he inspired a generation of young coworkers with his mystical love of Eretz Israel. Gordon wanted to create a "new Jew," one who was freed from commercial business and the professions, from the traditional middleman role in commerce that Christian society had historically imposed upon the Jews of Europe.

The very act of planting a tree in the land of Israel or removing a stone or gathering in a harvest was sacred. All were imbued with a life-giving force that liberated the Jew from the economic and psychological shackles of the Diaspora. Gordon's belief in the transcendent power of Jewish physical labor became an integral part of Israeli society.

Orthodox Marxism has traditionally viewed all forms of nationalism in negative terms, as tools of the ruling capitalist class to distract the workers from their own authentic concerns. Zionism, the Jewish nationalist movement, drew special scorn from Marxists. Marxists believed that the security and well-being of Jews could best be achieved through assimilation and class struggle which would end all forms of discrimination, religious hatred, and persecution. There were many Jews in the early years of the twentieth century and even later who subscribed to this tenet of Marxist ideology. But Ber Borochov (1881–1917) attempted during his brief lifetime to provide a Marxist rationale and foundation for Zionism. Borochov was another member of that remarkable generation of Russian Jews who supplied much of the intellectual and, as in A. D. Gordon's case, the physical power that was so necessary to create the Jewish state.

Borochov asserted that "genuine nationalism [such as Zionism] in no way obscured class consciousness." In fact, he pointed out, nationalism "manifests itself only among the progressive elements of oppressed nations." He called for a "proletarian Zionism" in which the oppressed Jewish workers of the world would build a true socialist society in Palestine that would be combined with Jewish "political independence." For Borochov, there was no conflict between Marxism and Jewish nationalism. Because Borochov was able to reconcile Marxism and Zionism in a brilliant intellectual tour de force, he became a guiding light for the left wing of Zionism.

By far the most controversial Zionist leader and thinker was Vladimir Jabotinsky (1880–1940). There has been renewed interest in Jabotinsky since the 1977 Israeli elections in which Menachem Begin became prime minister. Begin proudly calls Jabotinsky his political and spiritual mentor. Born in Odessa, Jabotinsky is best known as the leader of "revisionist Zionism," an intensely nationalistic and anti-socialist wing of the movement.

Jabotinsky proudly called himself and his group "maximalists," for they claimed both Palestine and present-day Jordan as part of the historic Jewish homeland. The original Palestine mandate area included this large area, but in 1922 the London government, led by Winston Churchill, detached the region east of the Jordan River (the East Bank) from Palestine. Jabotinsky, however, never accepted this unilateral British action and continually called for the establishment of an independent Jewish state on both sides of the Jordan River.

Jabotinsky considered himself the rightful heir of Herzl's "political Zionism," and his platform was straightforward, unambiguous, and utterly uncompromising: "The program is not complicated. The aim of Zionism is a Jewish state. The territory—both sides of the Jordan. The system—mass colonialization [immigration]. . . . The commandment of the hour—a new political campaign and the militarization of Jewish youth in Eretz Israel and the Diaspora." He organized a mass-membership youth group before World War II in Europe, and one of his followers in Poland was the young Menachem Begin.

During World War I, Jabotinsky, who never shrank from the use of physical force to achieve his aims, organized a "Jewish legion" within the British army. The legion fought with General Allenby in the Palestine campaign against the Turks in 1918. Following the war, Jabotinsky became increasingly anti-British as he saw England retreat from the pro-Zionist provisions of the Balfour Declaration.

Jabotinsky was constantly at odds with the established Zionist leadership of his time and finally organized his own movement, the "revisionists." This movement attracted a varied assortment of followers, including the novelist Arthur Koestler and Menachem Begin. The revisionists' unyielding territorial demands, their militaristic youth groups, and their basic opposition to socialism alarmed and angered the Zionist regulars. Consequently the revisionists remained a minority within the total Zionist movement.

But it was Jabotinsky's attitude toward the Arabs that perhaps aroused the most controversy. He denounced those Zionists who hid their real intentions from the Arabs. He was clear: the Arabs would have to become a minority within the Jewish state, but there would be "absolute equality" for all of its citizens. Jabotinsky was convinced that the Arabs would fight Zionism until an "iron wall" of

Jewish security was built. Then the Arabs would recognize that there was no hope of destroying the Jewish state, and they would finally have to accept its reality and deal with it.

In 1937, as the clouds of World War II were gathering and in one of Jewry's darkest hours, Jabotinsky testified before the British Royal Commission in London. He spoke for ninety minutes and, in a burst of emotion, declared:

> One fraction, one branch of that race [the Arabs], and not a big one, will have to live in someone else's state. Well, that is the case with all the mightiest nations of the world. I could hardly mention one of the big nations, having their states, mighty and powerful, who had not one branch in someone else's state. . . . It is quite understandable that the Arabs of Palestine would also prefer Palestine to be Arab state no. 4, no. 5, or no. 6. . . . But when the Arab claim is confronted with our Jewish demand to be saved, *it is like the claims of appetite versus the claims of starvation* [emphasis added].

No survey would be complete without a description of the life and teachings of Rabbi Abraham Isaac Kook (1865–1935), the leading exponent of "religious Zionism." Born in Eastern Europe, Rabbi Kook came to the land of Israel in 1904 when he was almost forty. In 1921 he was named chief rabbi of the Ashkenazi (European) Jewish community in Palestine. During his lifetime he became known throughout the Jewish world as "Rav Kook." *Rav* is an honorific Hebrew term of great respect, usually given only to a truly outstanding rabbi. Rav Kook decisively influenced a generation of Zionist thinkers, and his imprint remains on the state of Israel today.

Although he was a religious mystic, Kook's Zionist ideals emerge with great lucidity in his writings: "The hope for redemption is the force that sustains Judaism in the Diaspora; the Judaism of Eretz Israel is the very redemption. . . . Deep in the heart of every Jew, in its purest and holiest recesses, there blazes the fire of Israel. . . . The real and organic holiness of Jewry can become manifest only by the return of the people to its land." Rav Kook established a talmudic academy in Jerusalem, whose language of instruction was Hebrew. This action represented a clear break with many members of the Orthodox Jewish community who objected to the use of Hebrew in everyday life. They maintained that the sacred tongue could only be used in private prayer or in public worship. Yiddish, the vernacular of most East European Jews, was the usual language of Jewish schools, but Rav Kook's insistence on Hebrew helped legitimize and accelerate its acceptance in the land of Israel.

Rav Kook sought to bridge the gap between the observant and non-observant Jews of Palestine. He strongly believed that *all* of the Jews who lived in the land were partners in preparing the Jewish homeland and people for the "final redemption . . . the coming of the days of the Messiah." Rav Kook's personal piety and his all-inclusive religious message had an appeal far beyond the Orthodox community. His vision of a reborn Zion was not a narrow parochial one. Rather, he taught: "Our return will succeed only if it will be marked, along with its spiritual glory, by a physical return which will create healthy flesh and blood, strong and well-formed bodies, and a fiery spirit encased in powerful muscles. . . ."

The personality and career of Chaim Weizmann (1874–1952) dominated the entire Zionist movement from the death of Herzl until the birth of the state of Israel. Born in czarist Russia, Weizmann was a university chemistry professor who seemed to be present at almost every critical moment in Zionist history, beginning with his presence at the second Congress in 1898. Weizmann was an early follower of Herzl, but he also publicly disagreed with some of the founder's policies. In 1903, Herzl was willing to accept the British offer of Uganda as a possible "Jewish national home" instead of Palestine. Herzl believed the situation of the Jewish people was so desperate that almost any "legally secured" land could serve as a Jewish state. Weizmann, however, bitterly opposed the Uganda plan and insisted that only the historic land of Israel could be the site of the Jewish state. The Uganda proposal was defeated, and afterward all Zionist efforts were directed solely to rebuilding Eretz Israel.

In the years before World War I, Weizmann worked with Buber and others in emphasizing the "spiritual and cultural Zionism" of Ahad Ha'am. Weizmann moved to England in 1904 and became a faculty member at Manchester University, where his considerable personal grace and charm converted many English Christian leaders to the Zionist cause. One of his major successes in this effort was Arthur Balfour. As a chemist, Weizmann made a significant contribution to the British war effort against Germany in World War I and, as a Zionist, he was central in achieving the Balfour Declaration in 1917.

In 1918 and 1919, Weizmann carried on personal negotiations with Emir Faisal, the Arab leader. In 1920, Weizmann was elected president of the World Zionist Organization where he was constantly engaged in intra-Zionist battles, a favorite sport of the period. His internecine enemies at various times included Jabotinsky, United States Supreme Court Justice Louis Brandeis (a leading American Zionist), Abba Hillel Silver of Cleveland (an American Reform rabbi who was an ardent public advocate of Zionism), and David Ben-Gurion (the Yishuv's political leader in the 1930s and 1940s and the state of Israel's first prime minister). Yet Weizmann seemingly survived every battle and, with the passage of years and the diminution of his eyesight, his popularity rose. He served as Israel's first president, a largely honorary office, until his death in 1952.

Weizmann's Zionism was a mixture of traditional East European Jewish values, a pragmatic program of flexibility, and a deep affection and trust for Great Britain. His son, Michael, a Royal Air Force pilot, was killed in action during World War II. Weizmann wrote, "I have made it my work to explain the Jewish people to the British and the British people to the Jews." His Zionist critics, and there were many, felt that his overidentification with Great Britain, based in large part upon his 1917 success with the Balfour Declaration, had blinded him to the harsh and unjust British policies in mandate Palestine.

Weizmann was totally at home whether visiting a small Jewish village in Eastern Europe, negotiating with English prime ministers and Arab rulers, testifying before the United Nations in behalf of a Jewish state in Palestine, accepting the applause of young Jewish children on a kibbutz in Israel, or engaging in bitter conflict with his Zionist colleagues.

Weizmann's most painful and poignant moment came in 1937 when he urged the Zionist movement to accept the British concept of a partitioned Palestine, "the proposal to found a Jewish state in a reduced area of Eretz Israel." He broke down and openly wept during his speech before the Zionist Congress in Zurich, but he composed himself and concluded in pure Weizmann-like fashion:

The choice lies between a Jewish minority in the whole of Palestine or a compact Jewish state in part. . . . God has promised Eretz Israel to the Jews. This is our charter. But we are men of our own time with limited horizons, heavily laden with responsibility toward the generations to come. . . . We have to accept it . . . never in two thousand years has the responsibility been so great as now. . . . Fate has laid it upon us. . . . *We can only do the possible* . . . [emphasis added].

But the Middle East Arab leadership in 1937 rejected the principle of partition which Weizmann and ultimately the mainstream Zionist movement grudgingly accepted. It was a critical and far-reaching decision for both Jews and Arabs. One group was willing to divide and share the land it had claimed as totally its own. The other refused any compromise or division of the land it also called its own. These two divergent national policies have decisively shaped the Middle East ever since.

Ten years later, the United Nations General Assembly supported a Palestine partition plan, and again the Arabs rejected the call for a Jewish and an Arab state in Palestine. The Zionist leadership of 1947, however, accepted the UN plan and, in 1948, the independent Jewish state of Israel was officially declared. Weizmann's determined and pragmatic leadership of a decade earlier had established the principle of partition as an accepted doctrine of Zionism: "We can only do the possible."

Among the Zionist leaders of 1937 who had supported partition was David Ben-Gurion (1886–1973). Like Herzl, Ben-Gurion became a legend in his own lifetime, and it is often impossible to perceive his actual ideals and achievements. He is best remembered today for his unmistakable shock of white hair, his strong walnut-colored face, his open-necked shirts, and his dynamic style of political leadership. Born in Russia as David Green, he came to Palestine as a committed Zionist when he was only seventeen. Once there, he changed his name to the Hebrew "Ben-Gurion," ("son of a lion cub").

Ben-Gurion followed A. D. Gordon's "religion of labor" by performing physical labor on a Jewish agricultural settlement. But his writing and political skills were soon evident, and he rapidly became a leader of Palestine's Jewish community. Although Ben-Gurion was a foe of Jabotinsky, he served with him in the Jewish Legion during World War I.

Ben-Gurion remained a foremost exponent of socialist Zionism during his long life, and he proved to be a daring and resourceful prime minister of the fledgling state of Israel. He will forever be remembered as the man who, on May 14, 1948, in Tel Aviv first read aloud the Israeli Declaration of Independence. His voice announced to the world that the independent third Jewish commonwealth had been born.

David Ben-Gurion's ideas were a distillation of basic socialist Zionism and an intense mystical love of the land of Israel, especially the barren wilderness of the Negev, Israel's southern area. His home was a remote kibbutz, Sede-Boker, deep in the Negev where he is buried. His passion for the Hebrew language and the Bible was limitless, and his admirers often compared him to an ancient biblical prophet. He never shared Weizmann's affection or faith in Great Britain, and Ben-Gurion always insisted that no one country or group could or would give the Jewish people a state; only the Jews themselves by their own actions could create a Jewish state.

Ben-Gurion urged the Jews of the Diaspora to emigrate to Israel in order to fulfill themselves as Jews. He agreed with the rabbinic saying that it is better to dwell in the deserts of the land of Israel than to live in a palace abroad.

If Weizmann was a flexible pragmatist, Ben-Gurion was an absolute realist who clearly sensed that the Yishuv would have to fight a war to gain existence as an independent state. He understood the enormous difficulty of a small people asserting and maintaining national sovereignty in a world of *Realpolitik* and Arab economic power. As prime minister, one of his first actions was to disband the private Jewish fighting groups that had grown up during the British mandate. These forces were often the creation of a particular political group or party, and Ben-Gurion instinctively knew that there was no room in a democratic state for separate and politically oriented armed militias. The current tragic situation in Lebanon, with its hosts of armed groups, is a bloody and murderous confirmation that Ben-Gurion was correct. In the 1960s, he opened diplomatic relations between Israel and West Germany, the land of the Holocaust. It was a move that encountered stiff and vocal opposition both in Israel and in the Diaspora. Yet Ben-Gurion, ever the realist, knew that a viable Israel needed to relate to the most powerful and richest country in Western Europe.

His writings and personal life were characterized by utter simplicity. In 1944, in the darkest hour of modern Jewish history, Ben-Gurion outlined his basic Zionist philosophy to a group of young people in Palestine:

> The makers of the contemporary Jewish revolution have asserted: Resisting fate is not enough. We must master our fate, we must take our destiny into our own hands. . . . The fate of the Jewish revolution will be determined by its own inner forces. . . . The goal of our revolution: It is the complete ingathering of the exiles into a socialist Jewish state. . . . It does depend on us, on the Jewish people. . . . The meaning of the Jewish revolution is contained in one word— independence! Independence for the Jewish people in its homeland!

The brief overview of Zionism in this chapter indicates its extraordinary diversity. The movement has never been monolithic, nor have its leaders marched in a lock step of uniformity. Rather, Zionism is a highly complex national liberation movement that contains within it a wide range of political, religious, social, economic, and cultural ideas and policies. Zionism is a Jewish "tent of meeting" that has ample room under its roof for the deeply religious mysticism of Rav Kook as well as the "spiritual agnosticism" of Ahad Ha'am and the Marxist dialectic of Ber Borochov. It embraces the socialism of David Ben-Gurion, the rhapsodic "religion of labor" of A. D. Gordon, the democratic liberalism of Chaim Weizmann, and the charismatic political action of Theodor Herzl. Zionism also attempts to balance Martin Buber's "Hebrew humanism" and its call for a binational state with the militant nationalism of Vladimir Jabotinsky.

Like every other national movement, Zionism cannot be reduced to a mere slogan or catch phrase, nor is it fair or accurate to smear it with such malicious code words as "racist," "imperialist," "neocolonialist," or any of the other epithets that Zionism's enemies have hurled at it.

In recent years Zionism has been attacked by anti-Israel forces in the United Nations, mainly the Muslim and Soviet-bloc nations. Al-

most every year the UN endorses a sharply critical resolution of con-
demnation aimed at either Zionism or Israel. In February 1982, following Israel's decision to apply its administrative laws to the Golan
Heights, the General Assembly adopted a Syrian-sponsored resolution
that called for the "total isolation" of the Jewish state by the nations
of the world. This resolution was opposed by the United States and
almost every other Western or industrialized nation. The American
delegate to the UN, Jeane Kirkpatrick, reacted in anger to the UN
vote: "We are appalled by this resolution which distorts reality,
denies history, and inflames passions. . . . [It] will make peace harder
to achieve."

But despite these "distortions" and "denials of history," Zionism
and its creation, the state of Israel, endure. Its basic goal of reestab-
lishing and maintaining an independent and secure Jewish state in
the land of Israel remains unchanged. Its fundamental strength remains a moral one, a fact that is often lost in the world of global
politics and superpower rivalry. Every homecoming, especially one
after a long and painful separation, whether for an individual or for
a nation, is always difficult and sometimes misunderstood. Zionism,
the long-delayed homecoming of the Jewish people, is no exception
to this rule of life.

3 | *Holocaust*

The dark blue numbers are seen almost everywhere in Israel. The chief steward of my El Al flight had the tattooed numbers on his left arm, and one of the tourist guides in Jerusalem also bore the numbers. A passenger on a bus had the German word *Jude* ("Jew") etched into his skin along with his number. Nearly forty years after World War II, the numbers and the bitter memories remain for many Israelis.

"When the tattoo needle was stuck in my arm, I was no longer a person. I show the number to my children and grandchildren," one Holocaust survivor remarked. In their war against the Jews, the Nazis mocked the Jewish religious ritual of circumcision in which eight-day-old males enter into the covenant of Abraham, the patriarch. During the Holocaust, a new and demonic covenant of the flesh was brutally applied to millions of Jewish men and women: a dehumanizing prisoner number was burned forever into the skin.

Because the Holocaust, the systematic murder of six million European Jews by the Nazis between 1933 and 1945, was so monstrous, the Israeli Knesset (parliament) established a center in Jerusalem to commemorate the tragedy. The Knesset authorized the center to study and publish the history of the Holocaust and to honor the memory of the victims, their communities, and their organizations. The Israeli lawmakers designated the twenty-seventh day of the Hebrew month Nissan (late April) as an annual Holocaust Remembrance Day. What the Knesset members could not have known in 1953 was that the center would immediately become the world's most important and most haunting memorial to the Holocaust.

Called Yad Vashem, the center is a series of low, starkly simple buildings set on a West Jerusalem hill. It contains a Hall of Remembrance, a museum, synagogue, research center, library, and archives.

The center develops teaching material about the Holocaust for Israeli schools and collects eyewitness testimonies and other records from the Holocaust period. Its documentation aided the Israeli prosecution of Adolf Eichmann in the early 1960s, and it has provided evidence in other war-crime trials.

But Yad Vashem does something more. Six days a week the bright red and orange Israeli tour buses pull into its parking area where tourists from all over the world disembark to walk toward the museum. They are like tourists everywhere—colorfully dressed with sun hats and carrying expensive cameras while they carefully study their guidebooks. The visitors move swiftly, trying to do the day's sightseeing attraction as quickly as possible. But first they must walk along the "Avenue of the Righteous Gentiles" that leads to the museum.

More than three thousand non-Jewish men and women from all parts of Europe have been accorded recognition by Yad Vashem as "Righteous Gentiles." Such recognition is accorded only after a committee hears testimony and carefully examines the evidence. Each person so honored had at one time risked his or her life to save Jews from the Nazis. Many of the "Righteous Gentiles" have had trees planted in their honor along the approach to the Yad Vashem museum. Beside each tree is the person's name and country. Tourists inevitably slow up when they near the trees. "There aren't too many trees. Were there so few people who saved Jewish lives?" one tourist asks. Another remarks: "So many of the trees honor women. Were they more heroic than men?" The male tourists laugh nervously.

When the visitors reach the museum, they begin a journey unlike any other on earth. Yad Vashem chronologically displays the photographs, official documents, newspapers, and other records that tell the grim story of the rise of Nazism in Europe that culminated in the Holocaust. The museum also recounts the armed Jewish resistance to the Nazis both in the death camps and in the ghettos of some Eastern European cities. The captions accompanying the visual material are in Hebrew and English and are carefully understated. But it is all there—the yellow stars of David that Jews were forced to wear on their clothing, the minutes of the 1942 Nazi leadership conference that set in motion the murderous "final solution" to the so-called Jewish problem. There are pictures of the cheering Austrians welcoming Hitler to Vienna in 1938 as well as photos of the Jewish partisans who heroically fought the Germans in the European forests and countryside. And there are pictures from the Nazi death camps, including the hideous medical "experiments" performed on helpless Jewish prisoners, the shower rooms where lethal poison gas was sprayed on naked Jews, the crematoria where their bodies were burned, and the ghoulish collections of eyeglasses, artificial limbs, and even the hair of the victims. There are photographs of the emaciated survivors taken at the end of the war by the victorious Allies. Room after room at Yad Vashem present the documentary evidence of the Holocaust.

The Nazis recorded everything on film, and their photos are overwhelming. Why did they leave behind such an incriminating pictorial record of their atrocities? Did they believe they would never be caught? What the visitor to Yad Vashem sees are not snapshots, but extensive official photos. Were the Nazis merely good bureaucrats who desired comprehensive records to describe their actions? No, a more ominous answer slowly dawns on the visitor, and it is the worst answer of all. It is, however, the only one that makes any sense: the Nazis took pictures, kept meticulous records, and tattooed millions of people because they were proud of what they were doing. They believed in their campaign to rid the world of the Jewish people.

On my first visit to Yad Vashem, I concentrated on the faces of the victims, identifying with someone my own age or with someone remotely resembling members of my family. But in later visits I stared almost exclusively at the Nazis in the photographs, for they form an important part of the display. I was struck by their smirks, leers, and yes, their pride in what they were doing as soldiers rounding up Jewish prisoners, as doctors in their laboratories, and as death-camp guards. To view those grainy black-and-white photos taken in the 1940s is a shattering experience.

So shattering is Yad Vashem that every tourist group is reduced to utter silence as they move from one room to the next. People even stop whispering, and they physically disconnect from one another. Each person views the awesome displays alone. The silence in the museum is always startling as normally talkative children, including my own, are reduced to wide-eyed staring at the pictures. The captions are read and reread. "I went over every word," many say after leaving Yad Vashem.

When the visitors reach the most famous Holocaust photo, some people weep openly. It is a picture of a young Jewish boy, perhaps age eight or nine, dressed in a little overcoat and a small cap. He is walking past some heavily armed German soldiers in Warsaw in 1943. The boy's hands are raised in surrender, and his eyes are filled with terror. One of my daughters asks me in a hushed voice, "Where is his mommy and daddy?" I have my own questions that gnaw at me. "What were the Western democracies doing at the time? Where was God during the Holocaust?"

I am able to answer my first question thanks to some aerial photographs taken of the Auschwitz death camp in 1944 that are on display at Yad Vashem. At the time, the American and British Air Forces were bombing an I. G. Farben chemical factory that was located near Auschwitz in Poland. The Americans took some remarkable and all too revealing photos of the camp complex. The pictures clearly show the rail line that brought the prisoners to Auschwitz, the inmates' barracks, the electrified barbed-wire fences, the chimneys of the crematoria, and even the buildings that housed the deadly gas chambers. Incredibly, one can see prisoners arriving at Auschwitz by rail accompanied by their German guards, and there are other prisoners lined up in front of the shower houses: men, women, and children waiting to die, captured forever on film by a high-altitude camera.

Despite these photographs and the accurate intelligence reports about Auschwitz that reached the Allies, the death camp was never bombed. The rail line, headquarters, crematoria, warehouses, and roadways all remained untouched. Auschwitz was not considered a "military target," and its death machinery roared on intact until the war's end in 1945. Over three million Jews were murdered there. By not bombing Auschwitz, the Western Allies sent a clear message to the Nazis and to the doomed prisoners as well: "We know what is happening at Auschwitz, but we do not care to stop the killing, or even to slow it down."

The last display at Yad Vashem is the statistical record of the Holocaust. The pre-World War II Jewish population of each European country is listed alongside the number who were murdered. At first the numbers themselves stun the visitor: 6 million dead. It is something beyond the scope of human understanding, but in time a visitor notices that the statistical charts resemble the doors of the crematoria ovens. One woman, so struck with the display, said she actually "smelled the burning corpses." Such is the power of Yad Vashem.

Once outside the museum the dazzling Jerusalem sunlight is disorienting. The tourists are back in Israel, the land of the living, and conversations gradually resume. The visitors conclude their visit with a memorial service in the Hall of Remembrance next to the museum. Built of Jerusalem stones, the Hall resembles a tent or tabernacle. Like everything else at Yad Vashem it is understated. An eternal flame burns in the center of the Hall, surrounded by the names of the twenty-two largest Nazi death camps. The very names are chilling: Auschwitz, Bergen-Belsen, Buchenwald, Dachau, Treblinka....

As the Jewish prayer of mourning, the Kaddish, is recited, the sound of birds singing is heard inside the Hall. It forms a perfect counterpoint to the service. A Holocaust survivor has written that while she was in a death camp, she "marveled at a bird flying overhead, a lucky creature, far better off than I." The voices of the one and one-half million Jewish children who were killed in the Holocaust will never be heard, but we do have the sweet songs of the birds of Yad Vashem. The visit is over.

Today, every Israeli high school student receives thirty hours of Holocaust instruction. But educators have surprisingly discovered that there is insufficient teaching material available for Israeli teachers. Professor Yehuda Bauer, head of Holocaust Studies at the Hebrew University, sadly notes: "With little real knowledge of the Holocaust itself, the teacher, though concerned, is mostly perplexed. This confusion fails to satisfy the curiosity of our younger generation who have been stirred by what they see and read regarding the tragedy." Yad Vashem and other institutions are making efforts to overcome the shortage of appropriate educational material.

Although Israel is the world center for Holocaust studies, there is a growing interest in the subject throughout North America and Europe, even within the communist nations. There are many books, films, plays, TV programs, poems, and works of art reflecting this interest in the Holocaust. In both Holland and Denmark, the Holocaust is studied as part of these countries' national heritages.

In the United States, such Christian leaders as Professors Franklin Littell of Temple University in Philadelphia and John Pawlikowski of the Catholic Theological Union at Chicago have pioneered in bringing Holocaust studies to many Protestant and Catholic students. The National Conference of Christians and Jews annually prepares a Holocaust Remembrance Service that is used in nearly ten thousand American churches. "Holocaust Sunday" is now a regular part of the American Baptist churches' religious calendar.

But it is in Israel that the Holocaust has its most direct and personal impact. Some political leaders, including Prime Minister Menachem Begin, often base their actions and policies on lessons derived from the Holocaust period. The 1981 Israeli air raid on the Iraqi atomic reactor was strongly defended by Begin, who said that the raid prevented "another Holocaust of Jewish children." Young Israelis, especially native-born "sabras," react in varied ways to the Holocaust. Some are intensely curious and undertake an extensive Holocaust studies program. Others are outwardly indifferent, perhaps unable to face the grim facts. Both groups, however, reject the idea of Jewish powerlessness; hence the question asked by some Israeli children at Yad Vashem: "Where was the Israeli Army during the Holocaust? Why didn't it help?" Perhaps the youngsters are unaware that Israel did not achieve independence until 1948, three years after the end of World War II, and that during the Holocaust period the British severely curtailed Jewish emigration to Palestine. Other Western nations, including the United States, limited and sometimes barred Jews from entering their countries, in effect dooming them to Hitler's deadly "final solution." Nonetheless, Jewish powerlessness is inconceivable to many young Israelis. One sabra has written: "I have never known what it means to be a victim. Not ever. I cannot avoid thinking that a blessing."

But in June 1981, nearly five thousand older Jews who had been victims came to Jerusalem for the World Gathering of Jewish Holocaust Survivors. They came from forty countries "to celebrate life," and many brought their children and grandchildren with them. This first and probably last such gathering was a moving experience.

Death-camp inmates rediscovered each other after thirty-six years, some families were actually reunited after decades of separation, and even some kindergarten classmates from long-destroyed European Jewish communities found each other in Jerusalem. Computers were employed to locate lost families and friends. The gathering was climaxed with a service at the Western Wall where a proclamation was read by both Holocaust survivors and their children. The proclamation, delivered in Hebrew, Yiddish, English, French, Russian, and Ladino (the language of Sephardic Jews), resolved to keep the memory of the murdered six million alive and to work to prevent a future Holocaust.

Clearly, the Holocaust plays a key role in Israeli life, and it was also a powerful impetus toward the establishment of the state in 1948. The Holocaust, with its cadaver-like survivors, made a Jewish state an absolute necessity following World War II. Religious Jews today wonder if the timing of both events, the Holocaust and Israel's rebirth, was a coincidence or part of God's plan. "The magnitude of both defy logic," one Israeli told me.

It was a combination of guilt, disgust, and anger that spurred many Western political leaders to overcome the anti-Zionist policies of their own foreign ministries and state departments in the years 1945–1948. Those leaders also confronted centuries of latent and overt anti-Semitism in their countries as well as the strong pressure exerted by oil-rich Arab states who opposed the creation of a Jewish state. The specter of the Holocaust, the memory of the death camps, the Nuremberg war-crimes trials, the compelling demands of the Jewish survivors, and the shame of Western appeasement of Nazism were all at work as the six hundred fifty thousand Jews of Palestine moved toward political independence after World War II. So powerful was the Holocaust's impact that some observers contend that without the Holocaust, there would be no Israel today.

I believe it is both historically and morally wrong to perceive Israel merely as a "Holocaust state." Such a view turns Israel into an abnormality among the family of nations. Its natural, organic growth and its many acknowledged successes and admitted failures are either minimized or completely ignored. Instead, Israel is seen as a pariah state, a nation with a large blue number tattooed on its collective arm, a creation of the Holocaust. In such thinking, Israel is a defective state unnaturally born as a reaction to Nazism. Israel is a state to be tolerated, to be endured, and, worst of all, to be pitied.

Also, such a conclusion results in a bizarre equation: the murder of six million Jews has been fully indemnified by the emergence of Israel, with its 3.3 million Jewish citizens. The equation assumes the "slate is wiped clean"; the Jews suffered in Europe, but today they have a state of their own as compensation. Not only is the human arithmetic faulty, but the morality is contemptible.

The equation must be totally rejected. Israel is not some sort of trade-off for the evils of the Holocaust. The modern Zionist movement dramatically entered the world scene in the late nineteenth century with the convening of the first Zionist Congress in 1897 in Switzerland. The actual roots of Zionism are found in the Hebrew Bible and three thousand years of Jewish history. The 1897 Congress, called by Theodor Herzl, took place thirty-six years before the Nazis came to power in Germany. Among the many lies used by anti-Israel propagandists is the vicious canard that Herzl and Hitler once secretly met and reached an agreement: the Nazi persecution of the Jews would be intensified in order to help the Zionist movement achieve its goal of a Jewish state. This great lie, of course, has no basis in fact. The fact is that Herzl died in 1904 when Hitler was only fifteen. But the lie is still being spread and believed in some parts of the world.

Another misconception is that Zionism was created solely as a reaction to Nazism. The truth is that when Hitler became the German chancellor in 1933, the foundations of modern Israel were already well in place. National and communal institutions already existed, land reclamation projects were underway, kibbutzim were established, a trade-union movement was functioning, and a Jewish infrastructure of communications, culture, education, economics, and self-defense had been organized. Moreover, democratic political leadership had developed, and the revived Hebrew language was spoken by a Jewish population in Palestine that was growing steadily despite British and Arab opposition. In sum, an embryo state was already in existence in 1933.

I am convinced there would have been an Israel with or without the Holocaust. If the world had prevented the Holocaust, Israeli independence would have developed at a different pace, but it would have come. There still would have been intense Arab opposition, continuing Western anti-Semitism, and increasing global dependence on Arab oil. But an independent Jewish state would have reemerged on the world stage. The Jewish people, their human resources enlarged and strengthened by six million additional members and aided by supporters and allies throughout the world, would surely have found the ways and mustered the strength necessary to end nineteen hundred years of statelessness, of independence denied. Tragically, this thesis never had the opportunity to be tested. Hitler and his Nazi followers made sure of that.

4 | *Israel and the Arabs*

The incredibly complex relations between Israel and the Arabs of the Middle East are filled with claims and counterclaims, charges and countercharges, mutual recriminations, fears, stereotypes, hatreds, ignorance, propaganda, and, finally, sheer confusion. Facts and a balanced, fair approach to the entire issue seem in tragically short supply. Polarization is the rule and extremism the common currency. But an authentic understanding of Israel demands a clear and accurate look at this important question.

Israel, the Jewish state, must deal with four specific and separate Arab groups. First, there are the nearly six hundred thousand Arabs, about fifteen percent of the total Israeli population, who are full citizens of the state. The overwhelming majority of these Arabs, seventy-eight percent, are Sunni Muslims; about eight percent are Druses, members of a religious group that broke away from Islam in the eleventh century; and the remaining fourteen percent are Arab Christians. This Arab community remained in the land during the 1948–49 Israeli war of independence.

The second group is the more than one million Arabs who live in the Gaza district (363,000) and on the West Bank of the Jordan River (650,000). These two areas were originally part of mandate Palestine. But after the 1948–49 war, Egypt occupied Gaza, and Jordan took over the West Bank and East Jerusalem. In 1967, during the Six-Day War, Israel gained control of both regions. Israel officially calls the two areas "administered territories," while Arabs refer to them as "occupied lands." In 1977, when Menachem Begin became prime minister, the Israeli government began calling the West Bank by its ancient historic names: Judea and Samaria.

The third Arab group consists of the 1.5 million Palestinian Arabs who live in the neighboring states of Jordan (700,000), Lebanon

(400,000), Syria (180,000), Kuwait (120,000), Saudi Arabia (100,-000), and Egypt (20,000). Only Jordan has granted citizenship to the Palestinian Arabs. Since 1948, the rest of the Palestinians have remained stateless Arabs while living in Arab states. All Palestinian population figures are estimates, since no definitive census has been taken.

Finally, there are 116 million Arabs who live in the twenty member states of the Arab League, and the additional 41 million residents of Egypt, which was expelled from the Arab League because it concluded a peace treaty with Israel. The policies, actions, and attitudes of these four Arab groups toward Israel are all different depending upon geography, history, and national identity.

When the Israeli war of independence began in 1948, official British estimates placed the Jewish population of Palestine at 650,-000; the Arab figure for what eventually became Israel was put at 561,000. When the war ended a year later, the Arab population of the new state of Israel was only 140,000; this meant that 421,000 people had left Israel during the fighting. It was not long, however, before Arab leaders throughout the Middle East began claiming much larger figures, ranging from 1 million to even 2 million Arab refugees. Precisely why and under what conditions the nearly one-half million Arabs left is one of the most bitterly disputed issues of the entire Arab-Israeli conflict. Both sides have amassed a vast literature of official documents, statistics, eyewitness accounts, radio broadcasts, personal memoirs, and newspaper articles to explain what really happened in those fateful years of 1948 and 1949.

It is clear, however, that following the November 1947 United Nations vote in favor of the partition of Palestine, the fighting between Arabs and Jews sharply escalated throughout the country. At first the fighting was between armed Palestinian Arabs and the Jewish fighting forces of the Yishuv. But on May 15, 1948, the day after the state of Israel was declared, the armies of five Arab states—Egypt, Syria, Transjordan, Iraq, and Lebanon—invaded the new nation, fully expecting a quick military victory over the Jews. On that day Azzam Pasha, the Arab League's secretary-general, declared in Cairo: "This will be a war of extermination and a momentous massacre which will be spoken of like the Mongolian Massacre and the Crusades." Com-

ing just three years after the end of the Nazi Holocaust, Azzam Pasha's fearful prediction and the public threats of annihilation that were voiced by other Arab leaders drove the Jews of the nascent state of Israel into a desperate struggle for survival. The Israelis described their precarious situation with two Hebrew words: *ayn breirah*, that is, "there is no alternative" except to fight and win against overwhelming numerical odds.

During the turbulent spring and summer months of 1948, many Arabs of Palestine left their homes for a variety of reasons, and it is on this point that the dispute is most intense. The Arabs claim that the Israelis physically expelled hundreds of thousands of Palestinian Arabs from their homes, orchards, and farms. By their calculated actions, the Israelis created an unconscionable refugee problem, a problem that Arabs believe can only be solved by repatriation: all the refugees must be allowed to return.

The Arabs further charge that the Jewish state as proposed by the United Nations would have had a forty-five percent Arab population. Thus the expulsion of the Palestinian Arabs by the Israelis was necessary to guarantee a larger Jewish majority in the new state.

Israelis, of course, disagree with these charges. For example, Abba Eban, the former Israeli foreign minister, told the UN in 1957: "If there had been no war against Israel, with its consequent harvest of bloodshed, misery, panic, and flight, there would have been no Arab refugee problem today." Some Arabs admitted they left their homes to be out of the way of the Arab invasion armies. The Greek Catholic bishop of the Galilee, George Hakim, told a Beirut newspaper in 1948, even as the war was raging:

> The refugees had been confident that their absence from Palestine would not last long; that they would return within a few days— within a week or two; their leaders had promised them that the Arab armies would crush the "Zionist gangs" very quickly and there would be no need for panic or fear of a long exile.

But there was panic in many areas of Palestine, and the number of Arab refugees rapidly swelled. In October 1948, the independent and impartial London *Economist* confirmed that many Arabs fled because of "the announcements made over the air by the Higher Arab Executive urging the Arabs to evacuate. . . . It was clearly intimated that those Arabs who remained in Haifa and accepted Jewish protection would be regarded as renegades."

The events in Haifa, Israel's chief seaport, are especially poignant. Both Jews and Arabs agree that in April 1948 the city's mayor, Shabtai Levi, tearfully implored Haifa's Arabs not to leave. Posters in both Arabic and Hebrew were distributed throughout the city by the Worker's Council urging the Arabs to remain:

> Do not fear! Do not destroy your homes . . . do not block off your sources of livelihood and do not bring yourself tragedy by unnecessary evacuation. . . . By moving out you will be overtaken by poverty and humiliation. But in this city, yours and ours, Haifa, the gates are open for work, for life, and for peace, for you and your families.

But the appeals did not succeed, and many Arabs left mandate Palestine. Many fled because of fright, fear, or confusion, the tragic and inevitable result of every war in human history.

A much-disputed and controversial incident took place in April 1948, in the small Arab village of Deir Yassin near the vital Jerusalem-Tel Aviv road. At that time, a month before Israeli statehood was declared, there was no central Jewish military command, and two independent fighting groups, the Irgun and the "Stern Gang," attacked Deir Yassin. There was heavy fighting in the village, and the Arabs claim that the Jews killed over two hundred innocent civilians, many of them women and children. The Jewish account asserts that Deir Yassin was heavily defended by armed Palestinian Arabs who failed to evacuate the women and children from the strategically important village, which was an obvious military target. Nonetheless, the main Jewish leadership in Palestine strongly condemned the killings immediately after the incident.

Deir Yassin remains a bitterly disputed event around which many charges and countercharges continue to swirl. We may never know exactly what happened there in 1948, but the reality of Deir Yassin is far less significant than the meaning it has acquired in the Arab-Israeli conflict. Following the April 1948 battle, the very mention of the village's name was often enough to cause Arabs to flee from Palestine, even though the exodus had started earlier. Over the years the two words "Deir Yassin" have become a powerful cry for Arab revenge against Israel. On the other side, Menachem Begin has charged that the "myth" of the Deir Yassin "massacre" has been used by "Jew haters" throughout the world to undermine the state of Israel.

With the passage of time, the Arab refugee problem festered and the actual number of refugees was inflated. It remained unsolved, the Research Group for European Migration, an international body, charged, because it could be used as a "political means of pressure to get Israel wiped off the map or to get the greatest possible concessions."

A shift in the official Arab view of the refugee problem can be illustrated by the statements of Emile Ghoury, who in 1948 was the secretary of the Arab Higher Committee. In a September 1948 interview with the Beirut *Daily Telegram*, he said:

> I do not want to impugn anybody, but only to help the refugees. The fact that there are refugees is the direct consequence of the action of the Arab states in opposing partition and the Jewish state. The Arab states agreed upon this policy unanimously and they must share in the solution of the problem.

By 1960, however, in an address before a UN committee, Ghoury said: "It has been those [Israeli] acts of terror, accompanied by wholesale depredations, which caused the exodus of the Palestine Arabs."

Since the end of World War II, over 40 million refugees of various kinds have been resettled throughout the world. West Germany accepted nearly 10 million Germans, India and Pakistan exchanged 15 million Muslims and Hindus, France absorbed over 1 million refugees from Algeria, and the United States has legally admitted over a million Hungarians, Cubans, Chinese, Vietnamese, Cambodians, Soviet Jews, Haitians, Mexicans, and a host of other refugees. Yet the Arab refugee problem has remained unsolved since 1948. Elfan Rees, a World Council of Churches expert on refugee affairs, warned against repatriation as a possible solution to the problem. Along with many other refugee advisors, Rees urged instead the resettlement of the Arabs:

> I hold the view that, political issues aside, the Arab refugee problem is by far the easiest postwar refugee problem to solve by integration. By faith, language, by race and by social organization, they are indistinguishable from their fellows of their host countries. . . . There

is room for them, in Syria and Iraq. . . . Money remains unspent, not because these tragic people are strangers in a strange land, because they are not; not because there is not room for them to be established, because there is; but for political reasons.

As late as 1959, Dag Hammarskjöld, the UN's secretary general, proposed that the Arab refugees be resettled in the various Arab states. The funding for such permanent rehabilitation was to come from international philanthropy and from the oil revenues of the Middle East. Hammarskjöld's plan, however, was rejected by the Arab leadership. At the same time, Israel insisted that the resettlement of Arab refugees, not repatriation, was the best way to solve the problem. Nevertheless, in 1950 Israel offered to repatriate one hundred thousand refugees if the Arab states would take in the others. This offer was subsequently rejected by the Arab states.

The Jewish state has offered compensation for abandoned Arab property and has made over eleven thousand payments to Arab claimants. It is also reasonable to expect that the property of the seven hundred fifty thousand Jewish refugees who fled the Arab countries and came to Israel will have to be considered in any final settlement of the Middle East refugee problem.

But what of the one hundred forty thousand Arabs who remained in Israel during the 1948 fighting? They became citizens of Israel, living mainly in the towns and villages of the Galilee. Many of the wealthier and better-educated Arabs fled, and those who stayed came mostly from the lower rungs of the socioeconomic ladder. For nineteen years, from 1948 until the Six-Day War of 1967, the Arabs of Israel lived in a kind of hermetically sealed vacuum, almost in total isolation from their fellow Arabs who resided in neighboring states. The Arab states did not diplomatically recognize the Jewish state, and, except for Egypt, are technically still at war with Israel today. Israel's borders with Lebanon, Syria, Jordan, and Egypt remained tightly closed between 1948 and 1967, but the borders were never completely quiet. Arab irregulars frequently crossed the lines to attack Israeli property and civilians. These raiders were called *fedayeen* ("self-sacrificers") by the Arabs and "terrorists" by the Israelis. Acting in self-defense, Israel usually responded with vigorous military force and attacked the fedayeen bases across the borders in the Arab states.

The Arabs who remained in the new Jewish state made enormous gains in every area of their lives: health, education, employment, housing, and social welfare. Currently there are nearly seven hundred Arab educational institutions in Israel with more than one hundred seventy thousand students, fifteen times the 1948 figure, although the total Arab population grew only fourfold. Over one hundred ten thousand Arabs are in the Israeli work force. According to a U.S. State Department study, the "average per capita income among Arabs in Israel is probably higher than in any of the surrounding countries and is, in fact, higher than that of Jewish Israelis of Sephardic origin."

In 1966 the Israeli military authorities lifted all restrictions of movement for Arabs in certain border areas of the country, and the Arabs of Israel are not required to serve in the Israeli army since they may have to fight fellow Arabs, a clear clash of conscience. Nevertheless, Arab Druses do serve in the Israeli police and border units, and many Arab citizens donated blood for use during the 1956, 1967, and 1973 wars.

Under Israeli law, the Arab citizens suffer no de jure discrimination or legal obstacles. Indeed, the 1948 Israeli Declaration of Independence urged "the Arab inhabitants of the state of Israel to preserve the ways of peace and play their part in the development of the state, on the basis of full and equal citizenship and due representation in all its bodies and institutions. . . ." However, the Arab representation in the Israeli Knesset (parliament) is far below their fifteen percent of the national population, and their advancement into Israeli society has been much slower than for the Jewish citizens of Israel. There are social, cultural, and psychological disabilities, and clearly the Arabs of Israel are behind the Israeli Jews in many areas of national life.

Yet the Israeli government, sorely beset by high inflation, staggering defense budgets, serious international problems, and the continuing threat of war with several neighboring Arab states, does recognize that it must do more for its Arab citizens. The Arabs who live within the Jewish state, while perhaps preferring to live under some form of Arab sovereignty (and even this view is not unanimous), have not presented the Israeli government with a serious internal security problem, and there have been no armed uprisings or systematic campaigns of sabotage.

Israel has encouraged and maintained Arabic language schools, newspapers, and radio and TV programs. It remains official government policy "to integrate Israel's Arabs into all spheres of life: economic, cultural, and political." The status of the Arabs of Israel is a good barometer of relations between the two sectors of the total Israeli population.

The second group of Arabs lives next to Israel in the West Bank and Gaza Strip. Since the Six-Day War of 1967, Israel has administered these two nonconnecting areas that were originally part of mandate Palestine and historic Eretz Israel, the Jewish homeland. About one million Palestinian Arabs reside there. Immediately after the 1967 war, the late Moshe Dayan, then the Israeli defense minister, inaugurated the "open bridges" policy between Israel and Jordan. Tourists, workers, students, visitors, and goods all move peacefully across the Jordan River. Dayan's enlightened policy has permitted over 1.2 million Arabs to move freely between the two countries, and it has allowed Arabs to see Israeli Jews in everyday settings, free of distorted images and preconceived stereotypes. The Jordanians, however, have not extended the same privilege to Israeli Jews, and do not allow them to cross the bridge into their kingdom.

The Arabs of the West Bank and Gaza are not citizens of Israel; they retain their Jordanian and Egyptian passports. The final status of the two areas is yet to be negotiated since Gaza was never a part of Egypt (it was not returned to Cairo's control as part of the 1979 peace treaty), and the 1950 Jordanian annexation of the West Bank was not recognized by a single Arab state. Only two nations in the entire world, Pakistan and Great Britain, recognized the legitimacy of the Jordanian action.

Until a final peace settlement, Israel will continue to administer the West Bank and Gaza. Nearly seventy thousand Arabs from the West Bank and Gaza work daily in Israel, enjoying equal pay and the same social welfare benefits as Israeli citizens. As the West Bank and Gaza Arabs earn more, local industry has expanded. By all objective measurements, there has been a sharp qualitative and quantitative increase of agricultural, educational, health, welfare, and municipal services, and improvements ranging from personal income to cars, telephones, TV sets, energy consumption, travel, and university education. One illustration graphically illustrates the positive developments since 1967. In that year there were 3,930 classes for Arabs then living under Jordanian and Egyptian rule, and the total number of pupils was 134,859. By 1980 the two figures had risen to 7,420 classes and 264,069 students. The statistics for other areas of life are equally impressive, but the continuing reality of Israel as an occupying power remains.

The early Zionist leaders never envisioned a Jewish army of occupation, even one that attempts to follow the Israeli policy of "nonpresence and noninterference." The Zionist goal was to enable Jews to live freely and independently on their own land in their own state. The Jewish people were not to dominate the lives of other peoples. Increasingly, many thoughtful Israelis are deeply concerned about the possible negative effects that the prolonged occupation of the West Bank and Gaza may have upon the national character of the Jewish state.

Serious charges have been made that Israel has mistreated the Arabs of the West Bank and Gaza, and denied them their basic civil and human rights as guaranteed under the Geneva Conventions and the United Nations Declaration on Human Rights. In 1980, two West Bank lawyers prepared a study of the Israeli occupation for the International Commission of Jurists. It was highly critical of Israel and listed many alleged violations. The report, however, failed to acknowledge that Israel is still at war and, under international law (the doctrine of "belligerent occupation"), is entitled to disregard local law when military necessity demands it. Even positive reforms introduced by Israel are suspect. They are viewed by Arabs as part of a creeping Israeli annexation of the West Bank and Gaza.

The ICJ report brought an official reply from the Israeli section of the International Commission of Jurists. While acknowledging the difficult problems of an occupying power, the Israeli lawyers were satisfied that their nation has been legal and fair in its occupation policy. They claimed that military necessities and the need for public security and safety often dictate Israeli actions on the West Bank and Gaza.

Nevertheless, Israel has deported some West Bank leaders, including three city mayors. A former Israeli attorney general, and now a supreme court justice, has justified the deportations (there were six cases from 1976 to 1981) because of the deportees' anti-Israel "subversive activities." Some Arab houses have been sealed up or demolished by Israeli authorities. This action has been taken sparingly and with "extreme caution." Israel has charged that such houses "were used to prepare explosives . . . or as bases for the use of arms . . . when terrorist acts have resulted in the murder of innocent people."

The Israelis have sometimes temporarily closed Arab schools and colleges (there are four colleges on the West Bank) for a period of time. This has occurred when the authorities felt compelled to declare a state of emergency based upon a threat to public safety or security, usually as a result of anti-Israel, pro-PLO student actions and demonstrations. The schools have always been reopened, but the closings have served to exacerbate Arab-Israeli relations.

When the Israeli army gained control of the West Bank and Gaza in 1967, it inherited two sets of existing laws. One dated from the British mandate period, and the other laws were Jordanian regulations. Israel has kept both sets in operation but has introduced some legal reforms to the area. All neutral observers agree that Israel has carried out a relatively mild occupation since 1967, but it has been a difficult task for all of the parties concerned. The Palestinian Arabs of the region remain unsure and anxious about the final disposition of the West Bank and Gaza. Their lives and careers hang in a kind of limbo. Will Jordan regain control of the area? There was great opposition to Jordanian rule between 1948 and 1967. Severe measures were employed by the Amman regime to maintain law and order, and many West Bank Arabs do not want Jordanian rule again.

Will they become Israeli citizens? There is no enthusiasm for this anywhere on the West Bank or in Gaza. Nor do many Israelis desire an additional one million Arab citizens who would reduce the Jewish population of Israel to only sixty-five percent. Will the West Bank and Gaza Arabs form an independent Palestinian state? Former President Jimmy Carter revealed that Israel and many Arab States are adamantly opposed to the creation of such a state. Israel and Jordan are fearful that a Palestinian state situated between them will pose a direct threat to their national security. The other Arab countries view a Palestinian state as a radical and unstable force in the region, one that will be heavily armed and hostile to both Israel and Jordan.

The 1978 Camp David Accords between Israel and Egypt recognized the legitimate rights of the Palestinian Arabs of the West Bank and Gaza. But exactly what those rights include was never spelled out. Do they include total independence, full autonomy, political federation with Jordan, or an international trusteeship? No one knows, and a tense climate of uncertainty continues to pervade the West Bank and Gaza.

Tragically, the old pattern of political assassinations has repeated itself on the West Bank and Gaza. Prominent Palestinian Arab leaders who were called "traitors" or "Israeli collaborators" have been killed or wounded by PLO terrorists. It is a stressful and volatile situation, where almost every Israeli action ranging from tax collecting to police patrols is sharply criticized by some Arab leaders.

Former Israeli Supreme Court Justice Haim Cohn, a distinguished member of the International Commission of Jurists, has declared: "I am far from happy and complacent about certain aspects of the military administration . . . not everybody in Israel subscribes to the prevailing military concepts of security requirements, but . . . it cannot in fairness be denied that, in the history of military occupations throughout the world, the rule of law has never been better served and implemented than by affording the rights and remedies that Israel has made available to the residents of the administered territories [the West Bank and Gaza]."

The final status of these territories, therefore, remains in doubt, and the entire question of sovereignty is in dispute. In 1977, Cyrus Vance, then U.S. Secretary of State, said that "it is an open question as to who has legal right to the West Bank." Others, such as Yale Law School Professor Eugene Rostow, claim that Israel's occupation of the West Bank and Gaza in 1967 was a case of "legitimate self-defense" and that the Israelis have "a right to remain until a final peace is made."

Since the end of the Six-Day War, the Labor governments of Prime Ministers Golda Meir and Yitzhak Rabin, as well as the Likud government of Prime Minister Begin, have established nearly one hundred

Jewish settlements on the disputed West Bank, Gaza, and the Golan Heights. These settlements have a population of about fifteen thousand people. This settlement policy, which the American government has consistently opposed, has sparked enormous controversy both within Israel and in many other countries.

Israeli leaders, however, constantly remind their critics that the West Bank settlements are located in uninhabited regions, usually on state-owned land. When an attempt was made in 1979 to establish a Jewish settlement on privately owned Arab land, the Israeli Supreme Court rejected the plan. Most of the settlements are situated along the militarily strategic Jordan Valley or are close to the 1967 armistice lines which served as the de facto Israeli-Jordanian border for nineteen years until the Six-Day War in 1967.

All of the land west of the Jordan River is part of Eretz Israel, the historic land of Israel. However, many Israelis choose not to exercise their claims to the entire area if such restraint will advance the cause of a just and lasting peace. These Israelis would share the land with the Palestinian Arabs so long as Israel's legitimate security requirements are met and Israel retains its Jewish character.

The 1978 Camp David Accords deliberately left open the ultimate status of the West Bank and Gaza. William V. O'Brien, professor of Government at Georgetown University, asserts that these territories "must be considered today to be unallocated territory" and that "although the West Bank is 'occupied' by Israel, it is not at all clear that the area is occupied Jordanian territory."

There are other Israelis, however, who hold a different point of view. Most of the Jewish settlements on the West Bank have been founded by Israeli nationalists who are driven by a religious zeal to "strike roots" in all of Eretz Israel. Their actions have generally been supported by the Israeli government, and the entire question of the West Bank and Gaza has become a divisive issue within Israel.

Some Israelis claim that all efforts should go to building up the pre-1967 areas of Israel, such as the Galilee and the barren Negev. They charge that critically scarce financial and human resources have been drained away from these regions in favor of a string of Jewish settlements on occupied land. They further charge that the settlements may have to be abandoned when final peace comes to the area, not unlike the Sinai communities. Such a short-sighted policy, they assert, can result in great human and financial dislocation and waste.

Other Israelis cite compelling security needs and historic justifications for the settlements on the disputed land. They point out that international law is unclear about the West Bank and Gaza, and the Israeli claim is as legitimate, perhaps even more legitimate, than that of any other country. They further note that several Jewish communities existed on the West Bank before the 1948-49 war. These earlier Jewish settlements were overrun by Arab military forces, and many of the inhabitants were killed. Following the 1967 war, some of the sons and daughters of the dead Jewish settlers returned to the West Bank to reestablish their parents' destroyed communities.

An important point to bear in mind in any discussion of the settlements is the fact that between 1948 and 1967, when there were no Israeli settlements on the West Bank or Gaza, there still was no successful move toward peace. On the other hand, the Israeli settlements that were established in the Sinai peninsula after the 1967 war were no hindrance in achieving an Egyptian-Israeli peace treaty.

One other aspect of the settlement question needs to be addressed. Those who oppose the establishment of the settlements are saying in effect that the Jewish people do not have the right to live where they wish in Eretz Israel. In theory and in practice, a Jew should be permitted to live anywhere in the land.

Historically, there have been many Jewish communities throughout the land of Israel. In the final peace arrangements, the West Bank and Gaza may become part of a Palestinian state and/or Jordan. The Jews who reside in the area should have the choice of either returning to Israel or remaining in their existing communities, perhaps as Palestinian and/or Jordanian citizens.

To deny such a choice, as President Sadat did when he refused to allow any Jews to remain in the Sinai after it was returned to Egypt by Israel, is to guarantee that all present or future Arab states will be without Jews. Why must there be an end to Jewish life in Hebron, the site of the tombs of the biblical patriarchs and matriarchs? Why must Jewish life end in Shechem, the biblical name for present-day Nablus, and the site of Joseph's tomb? Or in Jericho, which is near the remains of a seventeen-hundred-year-old synagogue?

The third group of Arabs are the 1.5 million Palestinians who live outside of Israel, the West Bank, Gaza, and the Golan Heights. They reside mostly in Lebanon, Syria, Jordan, Kuwait, Saudi Arabia, and Egypt, and are perhaps the most bitter adversaries of the Jewish state today. These Palestinians are the aging, original refugees from the 1948-49 war as well as their children and grandchildren who have been born since then. Many still live in refugee camps in the various Arab host countries, and they have become political footballs in the Middle East. They are the victims of the unfulfilled promises made to them by Arab leaders since 1948, who claimed that the Arab nations would achieve a decisive military victory over Israel, "driving the Jews into the sea." This oft-promised triumph would then allow the returning Palestinians to reclaim their abandoned land and property, along with the land and property of the vanquished Israeli Jews.

The Arab victory has never come. The crushing defeat in the 1967 Six-Day War jolted the Arabs, and the Israeli successes in the 1973 war and in the 1982 campaign in Lebanon made it clear that Israel could not be militarily defeated. Since 1973, there has been a massive infusion of new and sophisticated weapons into Arab arsenals, but it still appears impossible for the Arab nations to destroy Israel "once and for all" by military means. Any attempt to do this would result in a catastrophic loss of Arab lives and the destruction of many cities, but still with no guarantee of a victory over Israel.

While the Palestinian Arabs were being deceived with false promises of a military conquest of Israel, the Israelis themselves welcomed and absorbed over seven hundred fifty thousand Jews from the Arab countries into their society. Although most Arabs do not want to talk about it, a kind of population exchange has taken place. Sabri Jiryis, of the Institute for Palestine Studies based in Beirut, admitted as much when in 1975 he wrote: "Each party must bear the consequences. Israel is absorbing the Jews of the Arab states; *the Arab states for their part must settle the Palestinians in their own midst and solve their own problems*" (emphasis added). Over the years the Palestinian Arabs, especially in Lebanon, have become an unstable element and a prime recruiting source for Arab terrorist groups.

For sixteen years, from 1948 to 1964, the Palestinian cause was presented to the world as basically a refugee question, one that called for international philanthropy, relief aid, and resettlement. Israel refused any large-scale repatriation of the Arab refugees pending the conclusion of a final peace treaty. Further, the return of the refugees to Israel would mean, as Abba Eban pointed out at the UN, that "hundreds of thousands of people would be introduced into a state whose existence they oppose, whose flag they despise and whose destruction they are resolved to seek. . . . Israel . . . is invited to add to its perils by the influx from hostile territories of masses of people steeped in the hatred of her existence."

In May 1964, the Arab League made a major strategic move away from a "refugee only" solution to the Palestinian problem by adding two new and potent elements: Palestinian nationalism and the call for the liberation of Palestine from "the Zionist occupation." Already in 1947 the UN had supported the creation of an Arab state alongside a Jewish state in mandate Palestine. But in 1964, the Arab League went far beyond the UN plan, calling for the destruction of the state of Israel and its replacement with an Arab state in *all* of Palestine.

To carry out this goal, the Arab League created and funded the Palestine Liberation Organization (PLO), whose aim is to eliminate the existing state of Israel by every means possible. The founding of the PLO in 1964 was a significant turning point in the Arab-Israeli conflict because it profoundly changed the basic Palestinian Arab strategy toward Zionism and Israel. That strategy, still operative today, has three main points. First, there can be no reconciliation or negotiation with the Jewish state because the Jewish people have no national rights; only the Palestinian Arabs possess such rights.

I was coleader of an interreligious delegation that visited Lebanon, Jordan, and Israel in 1974. It was a study trip sponsored by the National Council of Churches and the American Jewish Committee. During our visit to Beirut, we met with the PLO's Minister of Information, Yasir Abed Rabbou, at his headquarters. He rhetorically asked the group of American Christian and Jewish leaders: "Do Jews have the right, national rights, to the land of Palestine? No—in no way!"

The second basic PLO position follows from the first: because the Jewish people have no national rights, the Arabs are justified in pursuing a policy of total destruction of the Jewish state of Israel. During the Middle East journey by the interreligious delegation, Professor Muhammad Halej of the University of Jordan was asked whether Arabs could ever accept the principle of non-Arab sovereignty anywhere in the Middle East. He replied that Kurdish sovereignty might be tolerated, but not Jewish sovereignty in Palestine which is "the heart of the Arab world. Since we believe Palestine must be Arab, it has to be restored and reclaimed no matter how long it takes and no matter what the price. It's a question of 'dar al-Islam',* that which once was, must be again."

The third PLO position is that all actions or policies that conflict in any way with Palestinian Arab rights are inherently illegal and invalid. Elias Shoufani, the director of the Israel section for the Institute for Palestine Studies, has said: "All minorities in the Middle East . . . Jews and Christians, must be conformed to the Arab Muslim majority."

For the PLO, the inexorable clock of human history cannot be allowed to run when it comes to the Palestinian Arabs. Because they hold exclusive and total rights to the land of Palestine, the 1897 Zionist Congress program is invalid. The 1917 Balfour Declaration and the 1947 UN vote supporting partition are null and void. Israeli independence is illegal and must be ended, and the political and military results of the 1967 war must be negated. The 1978 Camp David Accords and the 1979 Egyptian-Israeli peace treaty are inoperative. Only Palestinian Arab demands are legitimate and valid; only those claims can be recognized and honored. All similar Jewish claims of national self-determination are illegitimate. Yehoshofat Harkabi, an Israeli specialist on Arab affairs, has summarized the problem:

> The problem was and remains . . . not recognition on our part of the Palestinians or their right to a section of the country, but the nonrecognition on the part of the Palestinians and the Arabs of our national right to a separate national existence of our own. In the Palestinian position there is a consistent fatalistic demand for exclusive possession.

That "fatalistic demand for exclusive possession" has helped bedevil Arab-Israeli relations.

*"Dar-al-Islam" ("the space of Islam")—those lands and areas that were once occupied by Arab Muslim armies in the sixth and seventh centuries.

The PLO has followed an "all or nothing" policy that calls for the destruction of Israel. In 1964, when the PLO was founded, the West Bank and Gaza were already "liberated" since they were at that time occupied by Jordan and Egypt, two Arab states. What, then, were the precise areas that the PLO was created to "liberate"? The answer is obvious—the area of mandate Palestine that constitutes the Jewish state of Israel. A PLO official told a Saudi newspaper in 1979: "We were not established in 1964 in order to liberate Hebron, Nablus, and Gaza, for those were already liberated [under Arab control], but rather we were established to liberate Jaffa, Haifa, Ramla and the Negev [all part of Israel]." Yasir Arafat has publicly stated the PLO's aim: "The goal of struggle is the end of Israel, and there can be no compromise."

The Palestine National Covenant (PNC) was formally adopted in 1968 and it has remained the official and most authoritative formulation of the PLO's program. The word "covenant" denotes the sacred character of the document. The PLO has spelled out its specific goals and strategy in the PNC's thirty-three articles.

Articles 1 and 2: "Palestine is an indivisible part of the Arab homeland . . . an integral regional unit." Palestine should not be divided into a Jewish and an Arab state. Articles 3 and 21: "The Palestinian Arab people possess the legal right to its homeland . . . it will exercise self-determination solely according to its own will and choice. . . ." The entire country belongs only to the Palestinian Arabs who will exercise total control over it.

Article 6: "Jews who were living permanently in Palestine until the beginning of the Zionist invasion (1917) will be considered Palestinians." The Jews who came to the land after 1917, the date of the Balfour Declaration, will not be Palestinians and must leave since they are aliens. Article 9: "Armed struggle . . . is the overall strategy, not merely a tactical phase." The radicalism inherent in this article rules out any political compromise or settlement with Israel.

Article 15: "The liberation of Palestine . . . aims at the elimination of Zionism." Another people's national movement must be destroyed to achieve Palestinian rights. Again, no negotiation with Israel is necessary or required. Article 18: "The liberation of Palestine from an international viewpoint is a defensive act . . . restoring the legal situation to Palestine. . . ." For the PLO, Israel's very existence is illegal and an international offense. Therefore, war against Israel is legal.

Article 19: "The partition of Palestine in 1947 and the establishment of Israel is fundamentally null and void. . . . " Article 20: "The claim of a historical and spiritual tie between Jews and Palestine does not tally with historical realities nor with the constituents of statehood in the true sense. Judaism as a religion of revelation is not a nationality with an independent existence. Likewise the Jews are not one people with an independent personality. . . . " Although the Palestinian Arabs vigorously demand the right of self-determination and self-definition for themselves, they deny those same rights to another group, the Jewish people. Every people has the right to define its own character and to shape its own distinctiveness, but this PNC article denies in a chauvinistic way those basic rights to the Jews. Harkabi notes: "The conception that the Jews do not constitute a national entity is a vital principle of the Arab position. For if the Israelis are a nation, then they have the right to self-determination, and the claim that only the Palestinian Arabs have the right of self-determination . . . is not valid." The Arabs have maintained that Israel is an "artificial entity," alien in nature, an illegal creation that must be destroyed.

Article 21: "The Palestinian Arab people . . . rejects every solution that is a substitute for the complete liberation of Palestine, and rejects all plans that aim at the settlement of the Palestine issue. . . . "

Since its founding, the PLO has gained world-wide attention with its many acts of armed terrorist attacks on civilians and its highly successful campaign to gain international acceptance and respectability. Currently over one hundred countries, mostly from the Third World and the Arab and Soviet blocs, as well as the UN, have granted the PLO diplomatic recognition.

In the period from June 1967 to the end of 1981, the PLO carried out over ten thousand armed attacks in Israel and abroad. More than one thousand people were killed and over six thousand were injured. Ironically, about one-third of the victims were Arabs.

Six of the ten thousand attacks stand out because they illustrate the type of targets that the PLO often seeks as well as the international character of its terrorism. In those years the PLO never attacked an Israeli military installation; all of its targets were civilians, thus tarnishing its campaign to pose as courageous "freedom fighters." In September 1970, the PLO hijacked and then blew up four Western jetliners. The PLO held the 600 passengers and crew members as hostages in a bleak Jordanian desert before releasing them. A few weeks later, as a direct result of this challenge to his authority, King Hussein expelled all the PLO forces from Jordan. It was a bloody intra-Arab battle, but Hussein was able to rid his kingdom of the PLO presence.

In May 1972, three Japanese members of the "Red Army" attacked a group of Puerto Rican Christian pilgrims in Israel's international airport. Twenty-six people were killed and seventy-six were wounded. The terrorists acted in behalf of the PLO which has links with other groups including the Italian Red Brigades, the South American Tupamaros, and the German Baader-Meinhof gang. In September 1972, the PLO seized members of the Israeli Olympic team in Munich. Eleven people were killed as the PLO brought terrorism and murder to this foremost international sporting event.

In May 1974, three PLO terrorists attacked and occupied an elementary school in the Israeli village of Maalot. Twenty-four people were killed and sixty-two were wounded, including innocent young schoolchildren. In July 1976, an Air France plane carrying 258 people bound from Israel to Europe was hijacked to Entebbe, Uganda. The hostages were freed in a daring raid by Israeli forces, but five people were killed and nine were wounded in the rescue effort. The PLO-trained terrorists included West Germans and South Americans. In March 1978, thirteen PLO terrorists using rubber boats came ashore on an Israeli beach from Lebanon and hijacked two buses and a taxi on the Haifa-Tel Aviv main highway. In a wild shootout with Israeli forces, thirty-three people were killed and eighty-two were injured.

The use of terrorism by the PLO has hardened Israel's resolve, and Israel has developed a fundamental response to PLO actions. It never yields to any PLO demands to exchange civilian hostages, even schoolchildren, for terrorists who are prisoners in Israeli jails. Since Israel does not have capital punishment even for murderers, there are over two thousand terrorists currently serving long-term prison sentences.

Almost every terrorist who enters Israel is killed by the security forces, and those who do survive are imprisoned. Following a PLO attack, Israel usually strikes at the Palestinian military camps or bases that are located in a neighboring Arab country. One such Israeli attack in July 1981 consisted of an air strike directed at the PLO's main headquarters in downtown Beirut. Unfortunately, there were many civilian casualties, and Israel was widely criticized throughout the world for its action. There was sharp criticism of this raid by Israelis and American Jews as well. In 1982 Israel moved into Lebanon to end the PLO attacks on Israeli civilians. Once again Israel was condemned for its actions. Despite the loss of innocent civilians, Israel believes there can be no appeasement of terrorism, and the PLO attacks cannot go unpunished. Israel's uncompromising stand against terrorism has served as a model for other nations like Italy and West Germany, who also face terrorism within their own borders.

The PLO's use of terror and its international connections with other such groups have destroyed its image as a peace-loving liberation movement. But the PLO has, however, made important advances on the diplomatic front, and it has effectively moved any discussion of the Palestinian Arabs away from a strictly refugee question to one of national self-determination. The PLO has convinced many people in the United States and Europe that it is the "sole legitimate representative" of the Palestinians, even though there have been no elections, referendums, or plebiscites to establish that fact.

The PLO's first major success came in the early 1970s with its call for a "secular democratic Palestinian state" where Muslims, Christians, and Jews would live together in harmony with shared equal rights. The words "secular democratic" have a positive resonance in the West, and for a time this idea was widely accepted by some American and European leaders as a viable solution to the Arab-Israeli conflict.

The "secular democratic state" balloon burst, however, when it was held up for critical scrutiny. Israel's 3.3 million Jews totally opposed the scheme. The claim that the PLO would be the instrument to create and govern such a state flew in the face of Arab history as well as the reality of every Arab state and society of today. Every Arab state, except Lebanon, has officially established Islam as the state religion. Lebanon itself has been virtually destroyed as a sovereign state, and a brutal civil war brought in an "Arab peacekeeping force" which was, in fact, a thirty-thousand strong Syrian army of occupation.

The gruesome spectacle of bloody Lebanon, where, since 1975, Arabs have daily killed fellow Arabs with reckless abandon, has not been lost on the Israeli public. They naturally ask: What would a triumphant PLO do to the defeated Jews of Israel? The tragic lesson of Lebanon, which once had a functioning legal system that protected the non-Muslim minorities such as Christians and Jews, has provided a horrifying answer to the Israeli question.

Since only the Palestinian Arabs would have the right to determine the nature of the proposed "secular democratic" state, the Jews at best would be dependent on the Palestinian Arab ruling authority. It would be a return to the historical condition of Jewish inferiority and subservience to Arabs, something that Zionism and the state of Israel were created to eliminate. The Greek Orthodox archbishop of Lebanon, George Khodr, declared that a "secular democratic" state would "have to be Arab in nature and texture." In January 1982, Arafat publicly articulated the PLO position: "Palestine is Arab. Arab. Arab. Arab. This land will speak no Hebrew."

After the breakup of Lebanon and the rise of Islamic extremism throughout the Middle East, the "secular democratic" state plan was no longer viable, and it has been replaced with another model: an independent West Bank/Gaza Palestinian state. Once again, many in the West have endorsed the idea that a small and disconnected state would satisfy Palestinian nationalist demands. Some PLO spokesmen have appeared in the Western media as "moderates" who support such a state. In 1979, Farouk Kadoumi, the head of the PLO's Political Department, told the Belgian press: "The PLO wants a just and lasting peace. This implies concessions from both sides. . . . " Three days later, the same Kadoumi was quoted in a Kuwaiti paper: "The PLO will not recognize Israel even if an independent Palestinian state is established." This PLO practice of saying one thing in the West and then contradicting it in the Arab world has been repeated often. Some top PLO leaders like Issam Sartawi have been fairly consistent in advocating a West Bank/Gaza state and PLO recognition of Israel, but the PLO still remains committed to "continue the battle and the armed struggle . . . liberating the entire homeland and the establishment of a national Palestinian state."

Israelis and most neutral observers believe a Palestinian state on the West Bank and Gaza would be heavily armed with weapons from the Soviet Union, but other nations would most likely want to sell sophisticated armaments to the PLO-controlled regime. Currently, the PLO receives $250 million a year from Arab countries, with Saudi Arabia providing one-third of that amount. A Riyadh newspaper has reminded the PLO that "Saudi Arabia pays for the bullets with which the Palestinians are fighting. . . . " A PLO state would quickly move to stamp out all opposition leaders and groups. It has already carried out a systematic campaign of political assassinations on the West Bank and Gaza as well as a series of murders of truly moderate Palestinian leaders in Europe. Yehoshua Arieli, a professor of History at Hebrew University and an Israeli "dove" (one who favors concessions by Israel to achieve peace with the Arabs), predicts:

> There will be a civil war . . . and the extremists will win. Then Arafat will expel the conservative notables on the West Bank. Then he will provoke Israel with attacks, incursions, and terrorist massacres. Then Israel will attack. We will have to retake the West Bank, and where will we be?

Nor would Israel be the only enemy of a PLO-controlled state. It would also press for the "liberation" of the eastern part of historic Palestine, the Kingdom of Jordan. Hussein's 1970 expulsion of the PLO from Jordan is called "Black September" by the Palestinians. The late Zuhair Muhsin, the former military head of the PLO, told a Dutch reporter in 1977: "After we have attained our rights in the whole of Palestine, we must not postpone, even for a single moment, the reunification of Jordan and Palestine."

The PLO itself is an umbrella group made up of nine different Palestinian organizations, each with a different leader and operational style. Some groups are directly controlled by Syria or Iraq, while the entire organization is led by Arafat, who also heads al-Fatah, the single largest PLO component. Though the funding and individual leadership may be different in each group, the central purpose of the

PLO remains the destruction of Israel. George Habash, a Christian Arab and physician, leads one of the most extreme Palestinian groups. He has declared: "They [the Palestinians] will continue the struggle until the destruction of the Jewish state—complete destruction and nothing less."

The PLO has been able to gain the support of such leaders as Chancellor Bruno Kreisky of Austria and former West German Chancellor Willy Brandt. Other political and religious leaders often meet with PLO officials, including Arafat, and come away from such meetings with the belief that the PLO is somehow easing its hard line or becoming more responsible. Such statements give legitimacy to the PLO's dual strategy—posing as "moderates" in the West while still continuing terrorist attacks on civilians. When such attacks take place, the PLO often shuns responsibility, claiming that "dissident" or "independent" Palestinian groups carried out the actions. When Israel responds militarily to such terrorism, it does so as a sovereign state fully responsible for its actions.

The PLO has assumed the psychologically rewarding role of the underdog in its confrontation with Israel. Israel's alleged human rights violations on the West Bank and Gaza and its policy of direct and powerful military responses to terrorism, with the sometimes unavoidable loss of innocent lives, have helped to gain support for the PLO cause. Even though it is well financed and well armed with modern Soviet weapons, the PLO still projects an image of a weak, dispossessed people in search only of justice and national liberation. This has led some in the West to believe that if there were a Middle East settlement along PLO lines, political stability would come to the region and the world's oil problem would be solved. Such thinking tends to overlook the various Middle East conflicts that are independent of the Arab-Israel confrontation: the Iraq-Iran war; the civil strife and violence in Lebanon; the socialist-monarchist, intra-Arab struggle; the Libyan-Egyptian dispute; the Islamic extremists who are active in every Arab country including Egypt, Syria, and Saudi Arabia. These extremists have already seized the Holy Mosque in Mecca, assassinated President Sadat of Egypt, and openly rebelled against the Syrian government. A capitulation to PLO demands would encourage the extremists, but it would not insure abundant oil supplies for the Western world or herald an age of political equilibrium in the Middle East. Elias Shoufani has said: "If Israel disappeared, the revolutionary fight would continue on other fronts."

A PLO victory would certainly mean the destruction of Israel as a sovereign, independent state ("politicide") and as a member of the family of nations. Some Western leaders, however, including former U.S. Presidents Ford and Carter, have urged America and Israel to negotiate directly with the PLO. The Israeli reaction to such proposals—cutting across all political, economic, social, and religious lines—has been negative. Again Professor Arieli: "For me the PLO means my physical extermination."

The U.S. government's position toward the PLO is quite clear. The PLO must make two substantive policy changes before any American recognition or negotiation is possible. First, the PLO must end all armed attacks both in Israel and throughout the world. Second, it must officially accept UN Security Council Resolution 242 of 1967 which affirms that "every state [has] the right to live in peace within secure and recognized boundaries free from threats or acts of force." The PLO must also state in clear and unambiguous terms that Israel is a legitimate state with a right to exist, and not an "artificial entity" or an outlaw creation. This would mean a fundamental reformulation of the Palestinian National Covenant.

When these two crucial conditions are met by the PLO, Israeli armed reprisals would end and an appropriate mechanism could be created to involve Israeli and Palestinian leaders in meaningful negotiations which would hopefully lead to a final and just peace agreement. The precise provisions of such a settlement cannot be predicted in advance, nor can outside parties or nations impose their own solutions. The process of direct negotiations will determine the ultimate solution to the Palestinian-Israeli conflict, but the process cannot even begin until and unless the PLO recognizes the permanent and legitimate existence of Israel as a Jewish state and until it ceases its international campaign of murder and terrorism. Many possible solutions and trial balloons have already been floated: Jordan as the Palestinians' state since sixty percent of its population is Palestinian and it is the eastern section of historic Palestine; a federation between Jordan and a Palestinian state; a "Benelux-type" consortium made up of Israel, Jordan, and a Palestinian state; a restoration of Jordanian authority on the West Bank, but with strong Palestinian self-rule;

full autonomy for the Palestinian Arabs on the West Bank and Gaza; and an international trusteeship in any area that is evacuated by Israel. The complex and vital questions of providing security for Israel and Jordan, possible demilitarized zones, borders, and a host of other critical issues would all be part of the negotiations.

The PLO, which has sometimes publicly hinted at recognizing Israel and then retreated under extremist pressure, must finally answer the most basic question of all: Will the PLO and the Palestinian people formally accept the independent sovereign Jewish state of Israel as a legitimate and permanent member of the family of nations? Or will it continue its announced policy as described in the PNC that seeks the total destruction of Israel by every possible means? A positive answer to the first question would be a quantum leap forward in the peace process.

Yasir Arafat, George Habash, and the other original PLO leaders have not achieved their goal of "liberating" Palestine or of creating a West Bank/Gaza state. Nor have they eased the human suffering of the Palestinian people, especially in Lebanon. Perhaps a new generation of leaders, more pragmatic and less tied to past failures, is needed to make peace with Israel and, by so doing, perhaps create an independent Palestinian state. The PLO needs leadership that can accept the de jure sharing of Eretz Israel/Palestine, just as Chaim Weizmann and David Ben-Gurion did for the Zionist movement in the 1930s and 1940s. As one Middle East observer put it: "The *only* way the Palestinians are going to get anything is by formally accepting Israel and the principle of two states. Since the Balfour Declaration in 1917, they have pursued an 'all or nothing' policy toward Zionism and Israel, and the Palestinians have always lost and come up with nothing." There is a clash of two rights, of two national movements, and both make ultimate claims for the entire land. One group, the Arabs, still seeks the annihilation of the other's national state and movement; they still officially deny the Jewish people's national rights. The overall goal must be maximum justice for both Jews and Arabs with a minimum of injustice—not an easy task, and one that will take accommodation, compromise, imagination, and courage.

The fourth and last group of Arabs are those who live in the twenty Arab League countries and Egypt. This group is the least problematic for Israel. The Egyptian-Israeli peace treaty has proven that mutual agreements are possible in the region. Negative attitudes, stereotypes, and caricatures have been hardened by decades of propaganda and bloody wars. However, such attitudes can be positively influenced and even changed once other peace treaties are in place. If the process can work in Egypt, the major Arab state, then the same process can work in Jordan, Syria, and Lebanon (provided there is a viable government in each country). Once a settlement is reached between Israel and the Palestinians, one that is perceived by all sides to be fair and just, then Israel can move to make peace with its immediate neighbors.

The other Arab states, even hard-line nations like Iraq, Libya, and Saudi Arabia, can then turn their attention away from Israel, and move to more constructive tasks such as internal national development and the improvement of their citizens' lives. Peace with Israel would remove the heavy, self-imposed burden of belligerency and war, and it would release enormous political and psychic energy for more constructive national tasks. The Arab economic boycott of Israel and Israeli-made products would be ended, as it already has been in Egypt. The anti-Israel boycott, which is illegal under U.S. law, is being ignored every day throughout the world. However, it still remains a disruptive factor in a world economy where nations and peoples are becoming more and more interdependent. The use of the boycott as an economic weapon against the Jewish state makes no sense since open and nonrestrictive trade benefits everyone, especially the millions of Arabs who still live in poverty despite the vast oil wealth of the Arab states.

Once Israel and its Arab neighbors have achieved a just settlement on the issues of borders, security, and refugees, they will both be liberated jointly to address economic questions as well. Together they could develop a mutually enriching program of regional cooperation involving communications, social and health concerns, science, education, culture, technical assistance, and tourism. Theodor Herzl once commented on his hope for a Jewish state, "If you will it, it is no dream." The same is true for achieving a just peace between Israel and its Arab neighbors.

5 | *Jerusalem*

Although the Hebrew name Y'*rushalayim* means "city of peace," Jerusalem has experienced more warfare, conquest, hatred, and strife than any other city. Jerusalem's geography helps explain its bloody history. The city sits atop a group of small, but strategically important hills, about twenty-six hundred feet above the Mediterranean Sea forty miles to the west. Just east of Jerusalem the hills fall sharply into the forbidding Judean wilderness, the traditional hiding place since ancient times for political and religious refugees. Young David hid from King Saul at Ein Gedi. Nine hundred years later, the religiously puritanical Essenes, weary of Jerusalem, fled to the Qumran caves near the Dead Sea, and a century after that Jesus confronted temptation on a lonely hill in the Judean wilderness. Control of Jerusalem is the key to the entire land of Israel.

Jerusalem's hills, though small in size, bear names that have stirred the souls and fired the imaginations of millions of people throughout the centuries. Mount Zion, just south of the walled Old City, is the biblical synonym for Jerusalem and is, according to Jewish tradition, the burial place of King David. The Jewish national liberation movement, Zionism, carries the mount's name. The Mount of Olives, just east of the Old City, has the largest and oldest Jewish cemetery in the world with graves dating back three thousand years. For Jews, the long awaited Messiah will come from the Mount of Olives and gloriously enter Jerusalem through the Old City's Golden Gate. In Christian tradition, Jesus will arise on the mount and majestically enter Jerusalem at the Second Coming.

Mount Scopus, on the northeast side of Jerusalem, derives its name from the Latin, meaning "observation point." For centuries this site has been a vital military approach to the city. Roman legions camped on Mount Scopus before conquering Jerusalem in A.D. 70, and in

1967 the Israelis captured the Old City from the same hill. It was the original home of the Hebrew University, founded in 1925, as well as the first site of the Hadassah Hospital. Between 1948 and 1967, following Israel's war of independence, the Israelis retained possession of Mount Scopus, while Jordan occupied the area surrounding it. During those years, the Jordanians did not permit Israel use of the Mount Scopus facilities, a violation of the 1949 armistice agreement between the two countries. Jordan's refusal to honor its promise compelled Israel to build an entirely new Hebrew University campus and Hadassah Medical Center in West Jerusalem. After the city was reunified in 1967, the original facilities were restored to use, and new buildings were added. Today Mount Scopus is again an integral part of the Israeli educational and medical systems.

Mount Herzl in West Jerusalem is named for modern Zionism's founder, Theodor Herzl, who died in 1904. He was buried in Vienna, but Herzl was so confident of his dream that his will stipulated his remains be brought to the new Jewish state after its independence had been achieved. Herzl's wish was honored in 1949, and today his grave occupies a prominent place on the mount that bears his name. Some Israeli leaders, including former Prime Minister Golda Meir, are buried nearby. However, most of the cemetery contains the graves of the many young soldiers who have lost their lives in Israel's all too frequent wars. It is only a few miles from Mount Zion to Mount Herzl, but the two hills span over three thousand years of Jewish history, and the military cemetery on the latter mount grimly marks the continuing human cost of maintaining Israeli independence.

Mount Moriah, within the Old City itself, is where Abraham offered his son Isaac to God as a sacrifice, and it is where the two Jewish Holy Temples were built. The Islamic tradition, deeply influenced by Judaism and Christianity, is also linked to Mount Moriah. Muslims believe the Prophet Muhammad was miraculously transported from Mecca to Jerusalem to the rock of Abraham's sacrifice on Mount Moriah. From there Muhammad made his nocturnal ascent to heaven on his winged horse, al-Buraq. Although the prophet never visited Jerusalem during his lifetime, the city ranks behind Mecca and Medina in religious sanctity for Muslims and is called in Arabic *al-Quds*, "the Holy One."

Omar, the Muslim caliph, captured Jerusalem in 638; fifty years later the magnificent Dome of the Rock was erected on Mount Moriah directly on top of the Jewish Temple site. Indeed, the Hebrew name for the Temple, Bayt ha Mikdash, became one of the Arabic designations for Jerusalem: *Beyt al-Makdis,* "the house of the sanctuary." Shortly thereafter, the *al-Aqsa* mosque, "the remote one," was also built on the Temple Mount near the Dome of the Rock. Thus, Islam has integrated Jerusalem into its own religious tradition.

Unlike the Islamic example of Jerusalem acquiring sacred status without Muhammad ever visiting the city, the Christian attachment exists because of specific events in the life and death of Jesus within Jerusalem. As the city of Jesus' resurrection and ascension into heaven, Jerusalem contains many holy places that trigger deep spiritual responses among Christians: Gethsemane, the Via Dolorosa, the Stations of the Cross, Golgotha, Calvary, the Church of the Holy Sepulcher, and the Garden Tomb. In the Middle Ages, Christians called Jerusalem *axis mundi,* "the center of the world," the city where the Passion took place, the city where salvational events unfolded, the actual place where Jesus walked, taught, was crucified by the Romans, and was resurrected. Jerusalem was also the scene of Pentecost, the birthday of the Christian church.

Jerusalem occupies a central role in much of Christian poetry, hymns, and prayers. For centuries, Western Christians came to the Holy City as pilgrims to retrace the steps of Jesus, to visit the holy places associated with his life and death, to walk in the Holy Land, and to pray in the Holy City. Generally, the Christian pilgrims came in peace; sometimes, however, they came as warriors. The Crusades with their record of rape, pillage, destruction, and bloodshed constitute one of Christianity's darkest chapters. In the twelfth century the Crusaders dominated Jerusalem and, during that time, massacred thousands of Jews and Muslims. But peaceful Christians also came to Jerusalem over the centuries to build schools, hospitals, libraries, and hospices. For many other Christians, no pilgrimage was needed since they were born in the Holy City as members of Eastern Orthodox churches.

Despite the historical attachment to the physical Jerusalem, Christian thinking has often focused on the heavenly Jerusalem, a universal, abstract, and purely spiritual concept devoid of specific territoriality and of flesh-and-blood reality. Such thinking denigrated the earthly Jerusalem, the real city. R. J. Zwi Werblowsky of the Hebrew University has observed: "To the extent that Jerusalem also has a terrestrial, geographical dimension as a holy city (for Christians), it is mainly in its quality as a memento of holy events that occurred at certain places—'holy places' therein." The emphasis on the heavenly city at the expense of the earthly one created a Christian ambivalence toward Jerusalem. Werblowsky notes: "A 'de-territorializing' tendency also asserted itself, and many of the great spiritual figures in the history of Christianity expressed doubts" about undertaking an actual journey to Jerusalem.

St. Augustine wrote: "When we thirst, then we should come—not with our feet, but rather with our feelings . . . it is one thing to wander with the body, a different thing to wander with the heart." St. Jerome was more explicit: "The heavenly sanctuary is open from Britain, no less than from Jerusalem, for the Kingdom of God is within you." And John Milton sarcastically describes the paradise of fools: "Here pilgrims roam, that stray'd so far to seek / In Golgotha him dead, who lives in Heav'n."

Christian ambivalence toward the two Jerusalems remains unresolved to this day. It has resulted in some serious political consequences that are usually expressed in contemporary Christian hostility to modern Israel's control of, and passion for, the earthly Jerusalem.

That Jewish passion is quite different from the Islamic and Christian connections to Jerusalem. The city decisively entered into Jewish self-consciousness when King David made it the political and religious capital of the Israelites in 980 B.C. Jerusalem's importance is enunciated in the prophetic writings and in the Book of Psalms. The city became both the symbol *and* the reality of the people and its God. Jerusalem is mentioned in the Hebrew Bible 750 times, and Zion 180 times. Nor did Jerusalem lose its transcendent importance when the Temple and the entire city were destroyed first by the Babylonians and later by the Romans.

Since the time of David, Jews have always lived in Jerusalem, except for the times when they were expelled by force. They tenaciously maintained their community in the city despite the many foreign conquests. It is beyond the scope of this book to describe in detail the central role of Jerusalem in Jewish liturgy, poetry, and writings. One Psalm, however, graphically describes the inextricable bond between the Jewish people and the city:

> By the rivers of Babylon, there we sat down, yea, we wept, when we remembered Zion.
>
> If I forget thee, O Jerusalem, let my right hand forget her cunning.
>
> If I do not remember thee, let my tongue cleave to the roof of my mouth; if I prefer not Jerusalem above my chief joy.
>
> Ps. 137:1,5,6, KJV

The Passover meal (Seder) concludes each year with the prayer, "Next year in Jerusalem." The daily grace after meals speaks of "rebuilding Jerusalem speedily and in our day." The Midrash says: "For sheer love of the earthly Jerusalem, God made Himself one above." This collection of ancient Jewish homiletical writings even has God declare: "But I will not enter the heavenly Jerusalem until I have entered the earthly one first." Clearly, there is no Jewish ambivalence about the two Jerusalems. The earthly, the real city, has absolute primacy. The Jewish tradition says that God granted the entire world only ten portions of beauty, and Jerusalem has nine of them!

For Jews, Jerusalem is no mere collection of holy places; instead, the entire city is sacred. Krister Stendahl, former dean of the Harvard Divinity School and one of the world's leading Christian scholars, has aptly written:

> For Christians and Muslims that term [holy sites] is an adequate expression of what matters. Here are sacred places, hallowed by the most holy events, here are the places for pilgrimage, the very focus of highest devotion.... But Judaism is different.... The sites sacred to Judaism have no shrines. Its religion is not tied to "sites," but to the land, not to what happened in Jerusalem, but to Jerusalem itself.

The story of Jerusalem itself has been recounted through the ages in almost every language of the world. The Hebrew Bible is the primary source of Jerusalem's early history. Forty years after David established the city as the Israelite capital, Solomon, his son, built the

Holy Temple that served as the religious center of the people until its destruction by the Babylonians in 586 B.C. The Israelites were exiled to Babylon (modern Iraq), but seventy years later the Second Temple was rebuilt when the Persian King Cyrus granted the Israelites permission to return to Zion.

Two hundred years later, Alexander the Great captured Jerusalem, but his large Hellenistic empire broke apart following his death. One of the post-Alexander factions was led by Antiochus, who attempted to eliminate all Jewish religious practices from Jerusalem and the land of Israel. Ritual circumcision was banned along with the study of Torah, and a statue of the Greek god Zeus was placed in the Temple. A Jewish armed rebellion against Antiochus, led by Judas Maccabeus, began in 168 B.C. Judas recaptured the Temple after three years of guerilla warfare and rededicated it to the worship of God. That rededication (*Hanukkah* in Hebrew) is celebrated annually as an eight-day holiday. The successful Maccabean revolt was the start of the second independent Jewish commonwealth (David's reign began the first), which reached its peak under King Herod, one of the master builders of all time.

During his rule, 41–4 B.C., Herod embellished the Temple, constructed a royal winter retreat and fortress on Massada (a bleak hilltop in the Judean wilderness), and built many architectural wonders. In A.D. 70, the Romans under Titus destroyed the Temple and crushed Jewish resistance on Massada. Later, the Romans brutally put down a series of Jewish revolts, most notably the Bar Kokba uprising in A.D. 135. In that year the Romans, in grand imperial fashion, renamed Jerusalem *Aelia Capitolina* ("the capital city"), and they expelled its Jewish residents.

Somehow overlooked by the Romans was the western rampart Temple wall built by Herod. It alone remained standing following the Roman destruction. The massive wall of large beige-colored stones became the focal point of Jewish yearning for a return to Jerusalem, for a restored independent commonwealth, and for an end to dispersion and exile. According to one mystical interpretation, God, like the Jews, was also exiled from Jerusalem, and the divine presence dwelt in mourning within the wall, waiting for the people to return. Jewish sadness was often expressed by tears at the wall, and in time the term "Wailing Wall" was given to the Herodian stones. Today in Israel it is correctly called *Ha Kotel ha Ma-aravi* ("The Western Wall"), and it is the most sacred place on earth for the Jewish people.

In 394 the Byzantine Christians who then controlled Jerusalem permitted Jews to return, though many already lived there in secret. The Arabs, under Omar, came to the city for the first time in 638, and the European-based Crusaders held Jerusalem from 1099 until their defeat by Saladin in 1187. In 1517 the Ottoman Turks captured the prize, and in 1540 Suleiman the Magnificent, an Ottoman ruler, rebuilt the Old City walls of Jerusalem. Those walls have now survived nearly four hundred fifty years of weather and warfare, not to mention millions of pilgrims and tourists.

During the Turkish rule, Jews returned to Jerusalem in increasing numbers to join the community already there. They came to pray at the Wall, to study at one of the many *yeshivot* (Jewish academies), to be near the graves of their loved ones on the Mount of Olives, and simply to live in the Jewish Quarter of the Old City, the oldest Jewish community in the world. By 1844 Jews were the largest single religious group in the city, and in 1872 they outnumbered the Christians and Muslims combined. The Jews became the majority in Jerusalem a quarter of a century before Herzl convened the first Zionist Congress in 1897.

In 1860 Jerusalem's Jewish population had grown so large that a new residence area was built outside the Old City for the first time in history. The past one hundred twenty years have seen the dramatic growth of many new neighborhoods in Jerusalem. But the Western Wall inside the ancient Jewish Quarter remained the focus of reverence. All synagogues in the world face Jerusalem, and all Jerusalem synagogues face toward the Wall.

The four-hundred-year Ottoman rule ended when British General Edmund Allenby captured Jerusalem in 1917 during World War I. As these things go, the British occupation was quite short-lived, lasting only three decades, but it was a tumultuous period. As Jewish and Arab nationalisms emerged in those years, Jerusalem became the center of intense conflict. Anti-Jewish riots erupted in the 1920s and 1930s. The latter were inspired by the Muslim Grand Mufti of Jerusalem, Haj Amin al-Huseini, who during World War II openly collaborated with the Nazis.

The British mandate period was filled with charges and countercharges. Jewish leaders accused the British of aiding and arming the Arabs, while the latter were convinced that Britain secretly favored the Jews. The British administration itself was often inept, malicious, insensitive (an Arab was appointed mayor of Jerusalem, ignoring the clear Jewish majority in the city), and, at its end, morally bankrupt. Nevertheless, despite fierce Arab opposition and a cruel British "White Paper" policy that severely limited Jewish emigration to Palestine during the 1930s and 1940s, the Jewish population of Jerusalem reached one hundred thousand by 1948.

When the Union Jack was lowered for the last time in Jerusalem in May 1948, ending the British mandate in Palestine, it was not replaced by a flag of yet another foreign occupying power, but rather by the blue and white Star of David of the third independent Jewish commonwealth, the state of Israel. It was clearly the end of foreign conquest and rule.

During the 1948 fighting, the Jews of Jerusalem were almost starved to death by an Arab blockade. The seige was lifted, but at a high human cost: about fifteen hundred men and women died to save Jerusalem. Based on the 1948 Jewish population of Israel, it was the equivalent of the United States today losing 571,000 people in a single military campaign! When the 1949 armistice ended the fighting, a new ordeal faced the Holy City. For the first time in its history, Jerusalem was physically divided into two separate and hostile sectors. The Jordanian Arab Legion, commanded by British General John Glubb, held the Old City and East Jerusalem with the important exception of Mount Scopus, while Israel controlled West Jerusalem.

The Jewish residents of the Old City were either expelled or taken prisoner by the Jordanians, and the ancient Jewish Quarter was ravaged. Fifty-five synagogues were destroyed, the Western Wall area became a slum, and many Jewish gravestones were removed from the Mount of Olives by the Arab Legion to construct the foundations, walls, and latrines of a military camp. For nineteen years Jerusalem was severed by barbed wire, mine fields, and concrete walls, and every year innocent civilians became the victims of the sporadic shooting that erupted across the border.

I first visited Jerusalem in July 1967 immediately after the city's reunification following the Six-Day War. I was shocked by the wrecked condition of the Jewish Quarter where former houses of worship and study lay in rubble with some buildings actually serving as stables for donkeys. My most poignant moment was walking through the Quarter and discovering children's school notebooks written in Hebrew in 1948 at the height of the fighting. The books were scattered under the debris and animal feces that had accumulated over nineteen years.

Today, however, the Jewish Quarter is totally rebuilt, a model of loving reconstruction. Jews again live there amidst flourishing synagogues, yeshivot, and community centers. For me the most vivid record of recent Jerusalem history is my photographs taken of the Quarter first in 1967 and again in 1981. The tremendous changes reflect the Jewish passion for Jerusalem and the eternal story of destruction, expulsion, return, and reconstruction.

Between 1948 and 1967 Jordan violated Article 8 of the armistice agreement that provided free access to the holy places and cultural institutions under its control. Jews were forbidden to visit the Western Wall, the Mount of Olives cemetery, Rachel's tomb in Bethlehem, and the Tomb of the Patriarchs in Hebron. They were also banned from using Mount Scopus's facilities. Jordan barred all Jews of the world, not only Israelis, from visiting their holy places. Israeli Muslims were not permitted to visit the Old City. One small concession, however, was given to Israeli Christians by Jordan: they were allowed to enter the Old City and its holy places on Christmas and Easter. Still, for nineteen years there was a ban on the acquisition of land by Christian churches in Jordanian-controlled Jerusalem, and Christian schools were required to give their students equal time in the Koran as well as in the Bible.

Following the reunification of the city, Israel abolished these restrictive laws. Today the holy places are open to all religious groups, and they are administered by the appropriate Jewish, Christian, and Muslim authorities. Israel's open access policy has been publicly praised by many Christian and Muslim leaders. It is a policy that guarantees freedom of religious expression, free movement throughout Jerusalem, and free access to the holy places for everyone. Even Israel's detractors and enemies have virtually ended their campaign against Israeli policy and practice regarding holy places. Too many fair-minded men and women from all over the globe have visited Jerusalem since 1967 and have seen the truth for themselves.

Another nagging issue needs to be put to rest. When the United Nations General Assembly voted in 1947 to partition Palestine into a Jewish and an Arab state, it also recommended that the entire city of Jerusalem be placed under international control as a *corpus separatum*. The Jewish leadership reluctantly accepted the UN plan in the hope the city might be spared conflict, but the Arab states opposed the recommendation for internationalization, claiming all of Jerusalem as an Arab city. However, the Arab position changed completely after Israel's military victory had left the Jewish state in possession of West Jerusalem and Mount Scopus. By 1949 every Arab state except one publicly endorsed internationalization. The lone exception was Jordan, the one Arab state that controlled the Old City. King Abdullah's representative told the UN that "my delegation believes that no form of internationalization . . . serves any purpose, as the holy places . . . are safe and secure, without the necessity for a special regime." Because of Jordan's opposition, the UN abandoned any plans to implement the internationalization recommendation.

It was only after the Israeli reunification of Jerusalem in 1967 that calls for internationalization were again heard. At first glance the plan may appear to be a sensible approach, but in fact it raises more questions than it answers and creates more problems than it solves. First, it has never successfully worked anywhere else. Berlin is a glaring example of the failure of internationalization, even with solemn promises by only *four* nations. The same four—the United States, the Soviet Union, Britain, and France—gave up their internationalized control of Vienna in 1955. The internationalized European city of Danzig of the 1930s was a disaster, and many believe that its abnormal status contributed to the start of World War II.

A city cannot be governed by an international committee. Every new road, sewage plant, school, hospital, or electrical power station would need approval from either group of nations or a UN bureaucracy. Who would finance internationalization? The dismal record of many UN members in meeting their fiscal obligations is not encouraging. Would the principle of a Big Power veto be invoked in

Jerusalem? If so, the Soviet Union, no respecter of religious liberty and human rights, would certainly play a destructive role in the city's day-to-day administration. Israel's recent experience with the UN has been traumatic, and there is no likelihood that the UN would be either impartial or effective in governing Jerusalem. Finally, and most important of all, the Jewish and Arab citizens of Jerusalem oppose internationalization. To impose an unworkable, unwanted, ineffective, and potentially dangerous scheme upon Jerusalem's residents runs counter to the oft-cited principle of self-determination. Internationalization would be yet another form of colonialism.

In 1947 the Vatican supported internationalization, but in recent years it has greatly modified its earlier position. Today the Vatican is calling for free access to the holy places, a viable Christian presence in Jerusalem, and international guarantees for the status of the city. The Vatican, however, owns only seventeen percent of the Christian holy places in Jerusalem. All of the other major Christian groups in the city—Greek Orthodox, Greek Catholic, Coptic, Armenian, and Ethiopian—oppose internationalization.

What often goes unnoticed in all of the discussions about Jerusalem is that it is a poor city with no industrial base. It has no harbor and only limited natural resources. An adequate water supply has been a perennial problem for over four thousand years, and Jerusalem has no nearby energy sources except the sun. Its current population of nearly four hundred thousand people makes it a medium-sized city, roughly equal to Portland, Oregon. Almost one of every four Jerusalemites (about ninety thousand) is enrolled in some type of school ranging from kindergarten to graduate studies at the Hebrew University. In addition, a large number of citizens are elderly or retired Jews who have prayed all their lives to come home at last to Jerusalem, the Holy City. Thus, the city has a small tax base and severe financial problems.

No one is more aware of Jerusalem's problems than its mayor since 1965, Teddy Kollek. He travels everywhere in the city without a bodyguard, and his home telephone number is listed in the directory. Kollek has been most responsive to Arab sensibilities, and even his critics give him high marks in this area. After the Six-Day War, Kollek organized an international Jerusalem committee composed of seventy well known architects, city planners, scholars, and artists. The committee serves as an advisory group to the mayor, and in 1968 it reacted negatively to a proposed "master plan" that would have demolished several existing neighborhoods, including a colorful out-door market, to build a new highway. Fortunately, the "master plan" was scrapped.

Kollek also established the Jerusalem Foundation, which raises private funds from around the world for the purpose of beautifying the city. Many of the new parks, gardens, and playgrounds of Jeru-salem were funded by the foundation. Under the mayor's direction, a lovely greenbelt has been planted around the Old City since 1967. The popular mayor operates with four main principles. First, there is universal and free access to all the Jerusalem holy places which are administered by their adherents. Second, there is unhindered develop-ment of the Arab way of life within the Arab sections of the city. Arabs are ensured religious, cultural, and commercial governance of their daily lives. This applies, of course, to Christians as well as Mus-lims. Third, there are equal governmental, municipal, and social serv-ices in all parts of Jerusalem. Finally, efforts are being made to in-crease social, cultural, and economic contacts among the varied communities that reside in the city.

Jerusalem today is a spectacularly beautiful city. The many new buildings by and large blend in with the existing older structures. The golden-colored stones used in almost every building give the city a gorgeous shimmering appearance, especially at sunrise and sunset. It is a compact city; within less than a square mile is the Western Wall, the Church of the Holy Sepulcher, and the Dome of the Rock —sacred space for Judaism, Christianity, and Islam. Despite the ten-sions of the Arab-Israeli conflict, Jerusalem is not a Belfast, nor is it a Berlin with an ugly and cruel dividing wall. Moreover, Jerusalem is safer than many American cities, particularly at night.

Mayor Kollek actively pursues a policy of maintaining Jerusalem's rich "mosaic" patterns of housing, language, religion, and education. There is no attempt to create a Middle Eastern melting pot, no efforts toward American-style integration. Rather, the city is like a radiant diamond with many prisms that refract and shine differently, one from another. It is not a smooth stone. Jerusalem is a collection of languages (Hebrew and Arabic being the chief ones), religions (Judaism, Christianity, and Islam—each one with many groups and diverse traditions), peoples (Jews and Arabs as well as Armenians, Greeks, Ethiopians, and even Chinese and Vietnamese). Not only do Jerusalem's citizens oppose internationalization, they also oppose any effort to integrate their city along Western lines. Teddy Kollek's gifted leadership has provided a bridge to reach the many parts that make up Jerusalem, and it all seems to work.

But what of the Arabs who make up twenty-five percent of the city's population? Their reactions have been varied. Everyone agrees that the Arab standard of living in Jerusalem, including the Old City, has substantially improved since 1967. The three-hundred-year-old sewage system has been upgraded, and there are new roads, schools, community centers, and social welfare programs. Arab per capita income has risen sharply since the city's reunification, but so have the taxes necessary for the increased municipal services. The economic statistics and my own conversations with Arabs confirm that theirs is a continually improving life style. But men and women do not live by bread, TV sets, flush toilets, refrigerators, or cars alone.

The owner of a leading Arab travel agency in East Jerusalem told me that he deeply resented the "Israeli occupation" but added that his business was good. He takes several trips a year to Europe and the United States, where he has many friends. Another Arab, who is building his own home, wants his house inside the city limits of Jerusalem and not on the neighboring West Bank. "I feel more secure in Jerusalem. Someday Israel may return part of the West Bank but never Jerusalem, and life for me and my family is good in the city," he said.

A more complex reaction is that of Pierre (not his real name). Born in Jerusalem and given a French name by his Arab-Christian parents, Pierre was educated in Roman Catholic mission schools in the city. Today he is a successful professional executive who works for a community institution in Jerusalem. Prior to 1967 he lived under Jordanian rule, but he never considered himself a real part of that nation. It is Israeli policy for all Arabs in East Jerusalem and on the West Bank to retain Jordanian citizenship status. Thus Pierre still carries Jordan's passport although he does not believe King Hussein's

Amman-based regime will ever return. Because of his religion and name, Pierre has suffered ridicule and abuse from his fellow Arabs who are Muslims. "The Khomeini revolution in Iran has created a fierce anti-attitude toward anything and anybody that is not Islamic: Judaism, Christianity, the West. They're all under attack now," he said.

Pierre is now in his mid-forties, married, and his four children (all with Arabic names) attend the same Roman Catholic school that he attended. Pierre emphatically rejects the PLO and its extremist, terrorist programs and actions. He respects Kollek's efforts to be a mayor for all of Jerusalem, but Pierre does not feel himself a part of Israel. By his own admission, he has a severe "identity crisis." "I seem to belong nowhere—not Jordan, not the PLO, not Israel—nowhere," he sadly remarked to me over lunch. Pierre feels he is representative of many Arabs in Jerusalem.

But Anwar Nuseibeh, another Jerusalemite, has no identity problem. He is a Palestinian nationalist who wants Jerusalem redivided again. Nuseibeh, a lawyer and a former member of the Jordanian parliament, also served as Amman's ambassador to London, Jordanian defense minister, and, before 1967, governor of Jerusalem. In 1977 he told J. Robert Moskin, an American journalist: "In Jerusalem (between 1948 and 1967) we had barbed wire, we had walls. But at least we felt we were not completely disinherited from a city we regarded as our own. . . . I do not accept Israeli occupation and annexation. . . . I do not recognize the laws of Israel . . . the Arab tradition (in Jerusalem) is like a tree that is withering. . . . We don't want an Arab city that consists of the weak, the needy, and the old. . . . The 1967 line was perhaps not ideal, but it is better than we have today. . . . " Nuseibeh speaks for those Arabs who want a redivided Jerusalem, but most Arabs want to maintain an open and united city.

What is the future for this jewel of cities? In all discussions for achieving a just and lasting peace in the region, Jerusalem is always placed last on the agenda. Jerusalem is not mentioned in the 1978 Camp David agreement between Egypt and Israel, and there is no mention in the peace treaty that followed. But Jerusalem, the real city, exists, and both Jews and Arabs agree that it is a key to peace.

There are three main parts to the solution of the complex problem that is Jerusalem. The first is the question of holy places. Israel has been a good and faithful steward since 1967, fully recognizing Christain and Muslim authority over their holy places. Second, the "mosaic" pattern of life is continuing in Jerusalem. The Israeli record in encouraging each group to maintain and deepen its own unique religious, cultural, and social life has, on the whole, been successful. Amidst the instability and turbulence of the Middle East, Jerusalem is an island of sanity, safety, and pluralism. There is no reason to think that this constructive policy will not be continued.

The final issue is the most difficult. Even with the best efforts of Kollek and others, the Arabs of Jerusalem refuse to participate in any political activity, though some have voted in municipal elections. Arabs refuse to serve on the city council or to hold any elective office in Jerusalem. Many are fearful that they will be attacked by the PLO if they do serve in any official capacity. Still, many Arabs do work for the city as civil servants, including work as police officers. Israelis are clearly prepared to make significant compromises to preserve Arab autonomy and the Arab life style in Jerusalem, as well as to ensure continued free access to the holy places. But no Israeli wants the city redivided again. Jerusalem is Israel's political capital as well as the spiritual center of the Jewish people, and Israel will continue to exercise full sovereignty over the city. Only the Jewish state has made Jerusalem its capital. On the two occasions the Arabs could have made the city their capital, they failed to do so. In the Middle Ages, they chose Ramla, a town near the Mediterranean coast, and in 1948 the Jordanians preferred Amman to Jerusalem.

Many proposals have been suggested to solve the sovereignty problem. The most interesting is Kollek's own borough plan based on the London model. Each borough in Jerusalem would have its own budget and autonomy over its municipal services and life style. Each borough would determine its own needs and priorities. Other plans foresee a shared city, the capital of both Israel and a future Palestinian state, a city with two flags but not divided. Others call for a city of "two cantons" in an Israeli-Jordanian and/or Palestinian confederation. Still others, like Anwar Nuseibeh, want the city repartitioned with separate passports, police departments, currency, and systems of government. Others speak of an undivided city with "shared sovereignty," but how this is to work has never been spelled out in detail. There is also the call for a demilitarized Jerusalem, except for the municipal police force. And the list goes on and on. The official U.S. government policy is that East Jerusalem is "occupied territory." Washington refuses to recognize Israel's 1967 annexation of the former Jordanian sector of the city, nor does the U.S. recognize the 1980 Israeli law that proclaimed Jerusalem the eternal capital of Israel under full Israeli sovereignty. The American Embassy has remained in Tel Aviv since Israel's founding in 1948, but a great deal of American-Israeli governmental business does, in fact, take place in Jerusalem. As the capital of the Jewish state, the city is the site of the Knesset (Israeli parliament), the president's official residence, the prime minister's office, the Ministry of Foreign Affairs, and a host of other government agencies and ministries. The National Museum and the Bank of Israel are also in Jerusalem.

Nonetheless, some American officials privately say that they would not be averse to a redivided city, but perhaps with Israel retaining the Jewish Quarter with its Western Wall. In such an arrangement, the reasoning goes, Israel would sacrifice part of its sovereignty in Jerusalem for the sake of a "real peace."

But any Israeli sovereignty in Jerusalem is unacceptable to Saudi Arabia's royal family. The Saudis assert that all of "Jerusalem is Arab," and it is impossible to visit the Dome of the Rock or the al-Aqsa mosque as long as they remain under "Zionist control." The fact is that anyone, including the king of Saudi Arabia, can come to Jerusalem at any time to pray. President Sadat of Egypt worshiped at al-Aqsa during his 1977 visit to Jerusalem. Ironically, during the nineteen years that Jordan controlled the Old City, the late King Faisal of Saudi Arabia never once journeyed to Jerusalem.

Mayor Kollek asserts that Israel "cannot and will not [give up sovereignty over Jerusalem]. This beautiful city is the heart and soul of the Jewish people. You cannot live without a heart and soul. If you want a simple word to symbolize all of Jewish history, that word would be Jerusalem."

My own conclusions are the following. First, Jerusalem must never be divided again. Nineteen years of division out of four thousand were bad enough. Second, the questions relating to holy places and to cultural, educational, and religious autonomy, as well as to the problems of administering Jerusalem, are all being solved by Israel in a constructive way. And finally, it makes good sense to defer any questions about Jerusalem's status until the end of the peace process. As a record of mutual trust and good faith (both of which are in extremely short supply in today's Middle East) builds up between Israel and the Arabs, a creative solution to the sovereignty question will be found, but it will not be a solution imposed on Jerusalem from the outside. Rather, the solution will emerge organically from the residents, who truly love the city.

In the meantime Teddy Kollek says:

> If, at worst, Muslim and Jewish differences prove irreconcilable, we will have to live in tension for a long time. All the more reason to care for the city as much as we can to ensure its welfare and well-being in spite of the strains and stresses. If, at best, Jews and Arabs find accommodations that are acceptable to the aspirations of all three faiths, no one would argue that what we have been doing for Jerusalem has been irrelevant.

6 | *Israel Behind the Headlines*

The American media—newspapers, magazines, radio, and television—have helped create somewhat of a distorted image of Israel's people. Israelis are portrayed as living in a perpetual state of tension, facing both murderous acts of PLO terrorism and the chilling specter of a full-scale war with hostile Arab neighbors. The media projects an Israel in extreme danger with the personal safety of its citizens in daily jeopardy. Many critics, some of whom have never visited Israel, have described the Jewish state as "an armed ghetto, a fierce garrison state." In 1981 one of America's leading news weeklies featured a cover portrait of Prime Minister Menachem Begin framed by a Star of David made of rifles.

Historical and geographical realities have, of course, compelled Israel to be most vigilant about its security, always keeping a careful watch on the policies and actions of the various Arab states and organizations. Every one of those states except for Egypt is still technically at war with Israel, even though it has been nearly thirty-five years since the conclusion of the 1948 fighting. In addition, the PLO's charter publicly calls for the destruction of Israel. When these factors are combined with the spiraling arms race in the region and the resurgence of Islamic religious extremism, Israelis have valid reasons to be intensely concerned about that most basic of human needs—physical survival.

But first-time visitors to Israel are always struck by the normality they encounter within the country. Concerts, museums, movies, plays, recitals, lectures, and bookstores abound in large number. Restaurants, coffee houses, shops, stores, and fast-food stands all compete for the visitor's attention. There are many taxis and private cars along with one of Israel's most common sights: bright red passenger buses. Indeed, the bus is a vital part of the total Israeli infrastructure. Buses

link the entire country in a vast system that is dependable, conven-
ient, and economical. Israel has only limited rail service, but the buses
seem to go everywhere. Even in the most isolated areas of the Negev
wilderness or on the desolate Golan Heights, there are many bus
stops—a comforting sight for the adventurous and often-fatigued
traveler.

Israel attracts well over one million visitors a year, and its hotels
are filled to capacity during the vacation and holiday seasons. There
is an enormous amount of new building construction throughout the
country, especially in the larger cities. Israelis crowd their streets as
they walk, ride, shop, drink, eat, talk, and look at one another. Clearly
all this does not fit the preconceived image of an embattled Israel
that lives behind metal shutters with its people afraid to walk the
streets. Israelis are simply not fearful prisoners in their own homes.

The weekly Jewish Sabbath (Shabbat) is a good time to observe
the people of Israel as they really are. Every nation has its own distinctive pace of public life, and the cadence of the world's only Jewish state is unique. The entire country slows down on Friday afternoon in preparation for the Shabbat that begins at sunset and lasts
until Saturday sundown. Most offices, restaurants, stores, banks, thea-
ters, and schools are closed. Newspapers are not published, and in
Jerusalem the city buses do not operate. Israelis generally remain at
home on the Sabbath, attend synagogue services, or participate in
leisure-time activities.

When the Shabbat ends on Saturday night, Israeli life dramatically
accelerates. Young people flock to the movies, discos, and coffee-
houses. Other Israelis line up for dinner at reopened restaurants, attend plays and lectures, or visit one another at home. Whether a
visitor is in Jerusalem—the Holy City, raucous Tel Aviv on the Mediterranean, the Red Sea resort and port of Eilat, or in the northern
Galilee town of Kiryat Shemona, the Saturday night scene is the
same. Israel celebrates a joyous public coming-out party every seven
days.

As the streets of Israel fill each week with its people, visitors ask:
"Who are the Israelis? How can they appear so normal in the face of
the unique vulnerability and hostility their nation faces?" The answers are surprising. Three of every four Israeli Jews were born either

in Israel or elsewhere in the Middle East. Over fifty-five percent of the country's Jewish population are native-born sabras, and another twenty percent come for Asian or African countries like Iraq, Morocco, Syria, Algeria, Tunisia, Yemen, Egypt, Turkey, and Iran. Only a quarter of Israel's Jews were born in Europe or the Western Hemisphere (the U.S., Canada, and South America). And with each passing year, the percentage of sabras increases. Finally, over sixty percent of the nearly 3.3 million Israeli Jews are of Afro-Asian background, called Orientals because of their Middle Eastern origins.

Israel's adversaries often charge that the Jewish state is a white European colony that was unfairly imposed on a homogeneous Arab Middle East by the Western nations as compensation for the Nazi Holocaust. Claims that Jews and the Jewish state are not an integral and authentic part of the Middle East, however, ignore the realities of Israel and the pluralism that is found throughout the entire region. The truth is that Israel is not only geographically situated in the Middle East, but its people are by birth, language, religion, and life style indigenous to the region.

I experienced this reality in a dramatic way in 1974 when I led a group of American Christian and Jewish leaders on a study-tour of Lebanon, Jordan, and Israel. One Saturday night we were in Beirut, and a week later we visited Jerusalem. I took many photographs in both capital cities and am constantly struck by the physical similarities of the Israelis and the Lebanese. Even today I still have difficulty distinguishing the faces of Beirut from those of Jerusalem.

Israel also conforms to the Middle East in another way: poor driving habits and excessive automobile accidents. Israelis blame their erratic driving on the worrisome "security situation," precisely the phrase we heard from equally reckless Lebanese drivers. Knowledgeable tourists report that Egyptians probably hold the world's record for accidents. Bad driving seems to be a common problem in the Middle East, and Israel, alas, is no exception.

When Israel became independent in 1948, there were only 650 thousand Jews in the country. One of the first official acts of the newly formed Israeli government was to open the country to unlimited Jewish immigration, the "ingathering of the exiles," a cornerstone of all Zionist aspirations and programs. During the first three years of Israel's independence, the nation's population doubled. This extraordinary feat of human absorption is the equivalent of the United States taking in 220 million poor immigrants within a three-year period. The newcomers to Israel, about 675 thousand in number, came from the displaced persons camps of post-Holocaust Europe and from ancient but persecuted Jewish communities in Arab countries.

This mass immigration placed an enormous strain upon the new Jewish state. Israel had just survived a bloody and costly war of independence in which one percent of its *entire* population was killed, the equal of the U.S. losing 2.2 million in one war! Israel was confronted by belligerent Arab neighbors, and her capital city was physically divided. Every newcomer required adequate food, clothing, and shelter, but much more was needed to absorb successfully the hundreds of thousands of penniless, dazed, and traumatized Jews who were "coming home to Zion." Every educational, medical, employment, communications, transportation, cultural, and psychological counseling facility was pushed to its limit to meet the critical human needs of the immigrants.

The frail Israeli economy was nearly crushed by the wave of newcomers between the years 1948 and 1951. One grim government austerity program after another was imposed upon the Israeli people. Shortages, rationing, and long lines of consumers were commonplace. Taxation quickly rose, soon making Israel one of the highest taxed nations in the world. The immigrants brought with them their own languages, styles of dress, diets, religious observances, cultural preferences, and family mores. For example, Jews from Morocco's remote Atlas Mountains or from isolated Yeman at the tip of the Arabian peninsula suddenly found themselves thrust into a twentieth-century society when they interacted with Jews from the "advanced" countries of Europe and North America. The native-born Israelis, the sabras, suddenly became a minority in their own land, although this quickly changed as the younger immigrants, especially those from Africa and Asia, established their own new and usually large families in Israel.

Mistakes were made in those early years of Israeli statehood. Well-intentioned social planners tried to settle all the newcomers together in newly created towns and villages or in hastily built urban neighborhoods. These schemes failed to acknowledge the importance of the country of origin among immigrants or the fact that people generally prefer to live among their own kind. Moroccan Jews, unsurprisingly, felt at home with other Jews who had come to Israel from Fez, Rabat, or Merrakesh, all Moroccan cities. The same feeling of affinity was present in every other immigrant group.

The kibbutz, with its highly structured and successful communal system of social services, housing, employment, and education, at first seemed a logical home for the penniless immigrants who arrived in Israel with little or no vocational training or skills. The kibbutz, it was believed, offered the best opportunity to absorb the newcomers, but the vast majority of the new Israelis preferred the more uncertain economic opportunities of Tel Aviv, Jerusalem, and Haifa. Very few joined kibbutzim.

Several comprehensive master plans were developed to settle the immigrants. Some of these plans worked well, and some failed. Israel has learned, as have the United States and other nations, that human beings do not always follow the social planners' carefully chosen blueprints.

Abstract terms like "total integration," "egalitarianism," and "overcoming ethnic differences" usually fail to become realities. But despite the acknowledged errors, Israel has welcomed and still welcomes every newcomer as the continuing fulfillment of the Zionist dream. Golda Meir publicly rejoiced at the ingathering of Jews from over seventy countries. "An Israel without them is not worth having," she said. Since the 1950s, Israel has developed more pragmatic and successful methods to achieve the difficult goal of blending a large number of newcomers into an existing society.

Like all complex societies, Israel has its share of generation gaps, polarizations, and ethnic rivalries. Two such problems illustrate the human problems facing Israel and the ways in which these problems are being addressed and hopefully solved.

One area of internal tension and polarization deals with the role of religion in Israeli public life. This ongoing problem has its roots in the very conception and purpose of the Jewish state. Zionism, the movement to regain Jewish sovereignty and independence in the land of Israel, contained many diverse elements and factions, with each one espousing a particular type of program and vision. Some Zionists were openly antireligious, skeptical of all supernatural theology, and alienated from traditional Jewish religious observances. Nonetheless, such Jews were deeply committed to "rebuilding Zion," generally along modern egalitarian socialist lines. In their Zionist vision, Jewish scientific, political, and cultural values would permeate a free and independent Jewish state.

This group provided much of the early leadership of the Zionist movement as well as of Israel itself after 1948. Such towering personalities as David Ben-Gurion, Chaim Weizmann, and Golda Meir fully appreciated the vital role of religion in maintaining Jewish solidarity and a sense of peoplehood throughout the many long centuries of statelessness. During those long years it was said that the sacred Torah scroll was the "portable Jewish homeland," but they were opposed to religious domination of Israeli public life.

The state-run system of elementary and secondary schools, the civil service, the army, and the public health services, although thoroughly Jewish in character, were never dominated by the precepts and practices of Orthodox Judaism. The Jewish religion was acknowledged as a major contributing factor in the development of the Israeli society, but it was never allowed to become the major influence in shaping public policies and laws.

In practice, each Israeli city, town, or kibbutz decides for itself what will be closed on the Shabbat. For example, buses do not run in Jerusalem on the Sabbath, but they do operate in Haifa. Autopsies, although forbidden by Jewish religious law, are performed when medically necessary and only with family permission. In addition to the general public school system, the state also supports religious schools in Israel, providing parents and students with educational options. Many Orthodox Jews want the Israeli legal system to be based exclusively on religious law, but they have been unsuccessful in achieving this goal. Israeli laws, though drawing heavily on the creative insights of the Talmud and other Jewish legal works, are based mostly on Western civil and criminal jurisprudence along with some laws that date back to both Ottoman Turkish rule in Palestine and the British mandate period.

The opposing groups in this ongoing dispute are usually called "secular" and "religious" Jews, terms that are both inaccurate and incomplete. Among all Jews, every aspect of life is potentially sacred, and nothing in the human experience is purely secular. The division between the two is an artificial one and has no real meaning within the Jewish historical experience. But semantic and theological inaccuracies aside, there is, in fact, a sharp division between those Jews who want Orthodox Judaism to be paramount in Israeli life and those who do not.

Strong and articulate advocates of Orthodox Judaism established their own Zionist organizations that later became Israeli political parties after 1948. Religious Zionists envisioned traditional Judaism's doctrines, laws, and practices as the foundation of a reborn Jewish state. In such a state the Jewish religion would move out of the synagogue and the home, its main focus for two thousand years, and enter into a total Jewish society. After all, the religious Zionists argued, what was the ultimate purpose and meaning of Jewish suffering, dispersion, and yearning for Zion, if not but to help create a thoroughly religious state where traditional Jews would be the majority in their own homeland? They feared a Jewish state devoid of Orthodox Judaism, but other Zionist leaders equally feared a Jewish state controlled by Orthodox Jews.

The problem is not unique to Israel, nor is it new in history. Beginning with the Emperor Constantine in A.D. 313, Christianity became the state religion of many European empires, nations, and states. It has only been in the last century or two that Western nations have attempted to separate religion from the state, and even today the lines of strict demarcation are often blurry or simply nonexistent.

Currently there are many states in which Islam is the officially established religion, by law and by practice. The recent chaotic and bloody upheavals in post-Shah Iran, including attacks on the non-Muslim religion of Judaism, Christianity, and Bahaism, are tragic examples of religious extremism gone wild. The attempt by Islamic fundamentalists to control exclusively every facet of Iran's public and private life vividly illustrates the intensity and persistence of traditional religious values in the twentieth century. Although President

Anwar Sadat of Egypt was a faithful Muslim, he was murdered by Islamic extremists who did not share his broader religious vision.

Closer to home, some American Christians regret that the nation's founders did not officially designate the new country a "Christian Republic, a Christian America." The long and often bitter struggle to maintain a separation of church and state in the United States is evidence of the tension and division within our own society. The historic battles over Sunday closing laws and Prohibition are manifestations of such polarization in American life. Today the complex issues of abortion, prayer in the public schools, and the growing controversy between adherents of human evolution and divine creationism are usually debated solely in religious versus nonreligious terms, a distinct disservice to both the issues and the people concerned.

Israel, then, joins many other nations in dealing with the vexing problem of striking a proper balance between religion and the state, a balance that has been severely tested in recent years.

The number of Orthodox Jews has grown in Israel and with that growth has come increased political power on both the local and national levels. There are three major religious political parties, and although their total vote in the 1981 elections was only 12.5 percent, their participation was necessary to form a viable coalition government headed by Menachem Begin. Although he is not a member of a religious party himself, Begin is quite traditional in his own personal religious practices and beliefs.

All of this has created a new assertiveness among Orthodox Jews. They have recently pressed the Israeli government on a number of sensitive and controversial issues including the prohibition of medical autopsies, the banning of all pork products in Israel, and the ending of flights on Shabbat by El Al, the Israeli national airline. Orthodox Jewish residents of Jerusalem have sometimes thrown stones at nonobservant Israelis who have driven their cars near Orthodox neighborhoods on Shabbat.

Ugly riots have broken out between Israeli police and those Jews who are opposed to the archaeological excavations near the Old City of Jerusalem. The Orthodox claim the site is an ancient Jewish cemetery and not merely historic public buildings worthy of scholarly study. The Israeli Supreme Court ruled that the archaeological explorations could go on.

The most serious dispute rages over the issues of personal status: marriage, divorce, and religious conversion. When Israel became a state in 1948, it inherited the "millet" system from the Ottoman Turks who had ruled the area from 1517 until 1917. Each "millet," or religious community, had independent and exclusive jurisdiction over its adherents in the areas of marriage and divorce. Even if Israeli authorities had wanted to change the millet system and introduce Western-style civil marriage and divorce into the country, the opposition from the Jewish, Christian, and Muslim communities would have been enormous. The domestic and international political price for such a radical change is simply too high for Israel to pay. In this regard, Israel is following yet another regional pattern, as there is no civil marriage or divorce in any other Middle Eastern country.

The Orthodox rabbinate in Israel has a monopoly on performing all Jewish weddings and in granting divorces. It also controls all conversions to Judaism within the country. Non-Orthodox Jewish groups, led by the Reform and Conservative movements, have sought to break this exclusive hold, but they have not been successful. Reform and Conservative leaders both in and out of Israel have been joined by many other Israelis who seek an end to the Orthodox control of the critical personal status issues.

Many conversions to Judaism that take place outside of Israel are conducted by Reform and Conservative rabbis. If, for example, one of those converts from the United States emigrates to Israel and seeks citizenship under the Law of Return, his or her request has usually been granted, in effect giving legal recognition to the non-Orthodox conversion. The Orthodox leadership in Israel wants to limit all such conversions to a strictly Orthodox definition and procedure, thus gaining total control of all conversions both in and out of Israel. The Reform and Conservative opposition has been sharp and widespread. The issue remains unresolved and continues to exacerbate relations inside Israel. *Time* magazine reported that Rabbi Alexander Schindler, the leader of America's Reform movement, told Prime Minister Begin that the "gates of the Auschwitz death camp were open" to all Jews, Orthodox and non-Orthodox. Surely, Schindler said, "the gates of Jerusalem" must be open to all Jews, both Orthodox and non-Orthodox.

In 1948, Ashkenazi (Western or European) Jews constituted

eighty-five percent of the Israeli population. They had a high literacy and academic level and a low birthrate, the usual characteristics of a developed society. Today the Ashkenazic percentage has dropped to forty percent, with Eastern or Afro-Asian (Sephardim) Jews now making up sixty percent of the population. About seven hundred fifty thousand Afro-Asian Jews have come to Israel from Arab countries since 1948, bringing with them a low literacy rate and a high birthrate, common traits of a developing society. Israel has made a concerted effort to raise the literacy rate of the Sephardim. The Education Ministry adopted a policy of placing Ashkenazic and Sephardic students in the same schools, but the student drop-out rate among the latter group has been high. Financial aid has been made available to assist children from large families to remain in school. Fifty percent of all Israeli children entering the first grade are of Oriental background, but the same group represents less than twenty percent of the university student population. As a small nation in both size and population, officials are acutely aware that Israel's future development and its national security are directly linked to maintaining an educated and technically skilled populace.

The need for adequate housing as well as quality education is another problem as Israel attempts to bridge the Ashkenazic-Oriental gap. In the early 1950s, thousands of newcomers to Israel were housed in *maabarot*, temporary transit camps. To meet the acute housing need, a large number of new apartments were rapidly built, and the maabarot camps soon disappeared. However, fifteen percent of Oriental Jewish families still have three or more people living in one room, twice the Ashkenazic percentage.

Bridging the intercommunal gap between Israeli Jews has been difficult, slow, and expensive both in human and fiscal terms, but significant progress has been made. These gains were made against the constant backdrop of overwhelming national defense and foreign policy concerns. "Objectively, if you look at the comparative statistics, we have very few poor and a high level of education compared with other societies. But that doesn't change the subjective feelings of those who are seen—and see themselves—as the 'Second Israel'," Professor Asher Arian, a political scientist at Tel Aviv University, has observed.

Leaders of the "Second Israel," the Oriental or Afro-Asian Jews, charge that their community has been neglected and shortchanged by the Israeli political and economic establishment, which is heavily Ashkenazi in its origin and socialist in its political expression. This establishment, the Labor Party, dominated Israeli politics without interruption from 1948 until 1977 when Menachem Begin's Likud Party first came to power. During those twenty-nine years, many Oriental Jews felt increasingly alienated from the Labor Party. In the 1981 national elections in which Likud narrowly edged Labor, over sixty-five percent of the Likud vote came from the Afro-Asian Jews, and seventy percent of Labor's vote was Ashkenazi, clear evidence of polarization.

Likud favors a laissez faire economic program that contrasts sharply with Labor's traditional socialist platform. Conventional political wisdom would have predicted the poorer Sephardic Jews voting Labor-Socialist as a means of bettering their economic status, while the wealthier Ashkenazi community would support the fiscal conservatism of Likud. Just the opposite was true as Likud's strong nationalism and its hard line on security and foreign affairs appealed to the Oriental Jews. The Labor Party was blamed, rightly or wrongly, for being insensitive and unresponsive to the pressing needs of the Oriental Jews. However, Professor Arian cautions, "Nobody has the Israeli voter in his pocket"—a sign of a functioning and healthy democracy.

Two important factors, one legal, the other personal, provide reasons for optimism as Israel struggles to bridge the gap between the Ashkenazi and Sephardic communities. First, although inequities do exist, there are no discriminatory laws or ordinances of any kind in Israel. Israeli officials consistently claim there is no discrimination "in law or in fact." Rather, they assert, there is a strong commitment to achieving national unity among all the Jews of Israel. There are no legal barriers facing Oriental Jews, nor is there a policy of favoring one group over another. However, more time, talent, and innovative programs are still needed to aid the "Second Israel."

Secondly, as one wit has remarked: "The East-West Jewish problem in Israel is being solved in North-South beds." Over twenty-five percent of all current Jewish weddings in Israel are between Ashkenazi and Sephardic Jews, and the figure is climbing. What were first called "intermarriages" are now commonplace. The president of Israel, Yitzhak Navon, is a seventh-generation Jerusalemite of Sephardic background, and his wife is a sabra of Eastern European origins. They call their children simply "Israeli."

Because there was no independent Jewish state from the year A.D. 70 until 1948, Israel has been compelled to play catch-up in nearly every sphere of national life. Nowhere is this more apparent than in the quest to achieve a sense of unity among the 3.3 million Jewish citizens. The extremely diverse Jewish population of Israel has come from over seventy countries of origin—the dramatic result of the "Ingathering of the Exiles." As the exiles came home to Israel, a critical question arose: How can a national unity be developed while still respecting the extraordinary pluralism of Israel's Jews?

No responsible leader seeks or even desires an Israeli melting pot that would reduce the population to its lowest common denominator by creating a static and stereotypic *homo Israeli*. Yet the negative and divisive results of nineteen hundred years of Jewish statelessness must be overcome if Israel is to solve its many domestic and international problems. This will demand imagination, determination, strength and daring—the same traits the Jewish people exhibited while maintaining their unique existence during the centuries of global dispersion. Israel has limited natural resources; its future growth as a nation rests with its people and their ability to forge an enduring national unity amidst diversity.

No one single person, family, or group can adequately represent the human richness of modern Israel, for its complex society is beyond facile generalizations or easy classifications. The country is an anthropologist's delight with its enormous variety of Jews and, given the nature of the Jewish historical experience, that diversity is in little danger of soon disappearing. Behind the daily headlines and the official population tables live very real people like the Lilker and Azoulay families. Clearly no two families can portray an entire nation, certainly not one as complex as Israel. Nonetheless, the Lilkers and the Azoulays accurately reflect some of the trends, attitudes, aspirations, fears, and hopes of Israeli society. Their stories, even in a brief form, provide us with helpful insight into contemporary Israel.

Shalom Lilker was born in Brooklyn, New York nearly fifty years ago. Following his graduation from Queens College, he entered the Hebrew Union College–Jewish Institute of Religion in Manhattan, Reform Judaism's rabbinical school. While there he married Shoshana Goldhaber, a HUC–JIR librarian. Shoshana was born in Jerusalem of Ashkenazi parents whose forefathers had come to Ottoman Palestine as youngsters to escape the deadly anti-Semitic pogroms of their native Eastern Europe. Shoshana received an intensive Orthodox Jewish upbringing in Jerusalem, and she moved to the U.S. in the late 1950s as a young woman to pursue her professional career.

Shalom, or "Shelly," as he is known to his family and friends, received his rabbinical ordination in 1959. During the next four years, he was a U.S. Army chaplain in Korea and a campus rabbi at the University of Texas in Austin. Many other young rabbis in those years followed similar paths, but in 1964, Shelly, Shoshana, and their two small children, Tamar and Ari, "made aliyah" to Israel. The Hebrew word *aliyah*, literally means "to go up" or "to ascend," and it is the traditional term used when a Jewish person moves from the Diaspora to settle permanently in Israel.

"Making aliyah" has deep religious meaning, for it is considered the fulfillment of a divine commandment. Jewish religious tradition finds profound significance in residing in the land of Israel. The *Zohar*, an ancient mystical work, proclaims: "Happy is he whose lot it is during his lifetime to live in the land of Israel, for such a person draws down the dew from heaven upon earth and whoever is attached to the land during his lifetime becomes attached ever afterwards to the heavenly Holy Land."

For twelve years the Lilker family has lived on a kibbutz (collective settlement) where Shoshana has continued her career as a librarian. For many of these years Shelly was a faculty member at the Israel Institute of Technology, the Technion, in the port city of Haifa, where he taught Israeli students American courses and technical English. But in 1980 he left university teaching to become the *mazkir*, or general secretary, of his kibbutz, K'far Ha-Macabi, located about ten miles from Haifa.

Since making aliyah, Shelly has mastered modern Hebrew, become an Israeli citizen, served in the Israeli Army's medical corps, and watched his two children become fully absorbed into K'far Ha-Macabi as true "kibbutzniks."

Although Shoshana is a sabra, a native-born Israeli, the move to the kibbutz presented her with special challenges as well. Her childhood years in Jerusalem were shaped by her family's Orthodox Judaism and the urban life of the city. During the Arab siege of Jerusalem in 1948, young Shoshana was a message runner for the Israeli military forces. Living at K'far Ha-Macabi with 350 other kibbutz members has been a startling change for her. While Shoshana's sister has remained in Jerusalem within the Orthodox religious community, Shoshana has had to adapt to a new set of realities at the kibbutz.

At first K'far Ha-Macabi was as strange for her as it was for her American-born husband. The kibbutz is a unique Israeli institution that has drawn world attention, and many books have been written about the *kibbutzim* (the Hebrew plural form of kibbutz). Can people live, work, and create together in a close society based on cooperation and shared ownership rather than on economic competition and the accumulation of personal profits and individually owned property? The kibbutz movement is now entering its fourth generation of existence. There are approximately two hundred fifty of them in Israel varying in size from two hundred to over two thousand members. The total kibbutz population is one hundred fifteen thousand, about three percent of the Israeli Jewish population. Despite its small numbers, the kibbutzim have produced many of Israel's foremost leaders including former Prime Ministers David Ben-Gurion, Golda Meir, and Levi Eshkol, as well as such national leaders as Yigal Allon. The kibbutz movement has also shaped Israeli society with its ideals of self-sufficiency, egalitarianism, and love of land.

The first collective settlement, or kibbutz, Deganya, was established in 1909 near the Sea of Galilee. At that time the area was a swampy marsh well below sea level, a fertile ground for malaria and typhoid fever and heavily infested with mosquitos. Deganya's founders were idealistic young men and women who were fired by the Zionist dream of creating a new kind of Jew in the ancient homeland. They drained the swamps, planted eucalyptus trees, and created a beautiful and productive settlement. Today Deganya flourishes and is on almost every tourist itinerary. Other kibbutzim soon followed

Deganya. They were usually situated on barren rocky soil, near swamps, or in the lonely Judean wilderness.

The energizing concept of the Jew returning to the Holy Land was a radical method of shaking off the debilitating effects of the Diaspora. For centuries Jews have lived by sufferance in pogrom-ridden, anti-Semitic lands, especially Eastern Europe. The kibbutz movement evoked an almost mystical response among its early members. Every tree planted in those early days of the kibbutzim, every rock removed by hand from neglected or abandoned fields, every seed carefully placed in the homeland's soil, every young farm animal lovingly nurtured, every fruit and vegetable joyously harvested, every pond painstakingly stocked with fish, every swamp that was drained and reclaimed for farming, every chicken or turkey that was added to the kibbutzim, every well that was dug for fresh water, indeed, every creative activity of kibbutz life was endowed with *avodah*, a Hebrew term meaning both physical labor *and* the worship of God. Inspiring songs were sung around countless kibbutz campfires in the heady early days of the movement. Those songs have entered into the national consciousness of modern Israel and retain their power to stir deep emotions. The early kibbutz movement was an explosion of pent-up Jewish energy and passion. Work on a kibbutz, on the land, was a self-liberating experience.

For centuries Jews were not permitted to own land in most Christian and Muslim countries. Jews were barred from becoming farmers or artisans and were often forbidden from even owning a horse for travel or a weapon for self-defense. Forced by medieval law to live in crowded urban and dank ghettos, Jews were compelled to perform the necessary but despised task of their host societies, for example, tax collecting and moneylending. For centuries the Jews were both de facto and de jure, a pariah people living an unnatural existence, highly vulnerable to religious bigotry and political persecution. It was an abnormal situation that threatened to destroy the internal self-confidence and self-esteem of the Jewish people. The Jews, however, were sustained by the radiant hope of a physical return to the soil of the land of Israel. Many of the religious holidays of Judaism are agricultural in origin (Sukkot—Fall Harvest of Tabernacles; Shavuot—Spring Harvest of Weeks; Pesach—Passover; Tu B'Shevat—

Arbor Day) and are directly linked to the changing seasons of the Holy Land. The Jewish people, although the spiritual and physical descendents of ancient farmers, vineyard keepers, and shepherds, were totally cut off from the comforting rhythm and cadence of nature in the land of the Bible. It was as if many beautiful plants and flowers had been forcibly removed from their life-giving soil and roots. That the cut flowers and plants managed to survive for nearly nineteen centuries is amazing, and that they have been successfully replanted in their ancestral soil is for many people a cause of wonderment and rejoicing.

The kibbutz was a dramatic, almost desperate, attempt to restore the Jew to the land within an agricultural community based on collective ownership of property, social justice, and full equality. The kibbutz grew organically out of the inherent needs of an emergent society and as a reaction to the compelling demands of Jewish history. Other societies, including the United States and the Soviet Union, have attempted to establish communal, even utopian, settlements. In the USSR they have been sponsored and controlled by the government, while in America they have usually been the dream of idealistic youth or older visionaries. Yet, almost every communal experiment has failed to survive throughout the world. Israel's kibbutzim, though only a small part of the total national population, have survived. Why did they succeed in Israel and fail everywhere else? Perhaps the Lilkers' successful absorption into K'far Ha-Macabi provides some answers.

The Lilker family lives in a small, compact, one-story building that houses another kibbutz family as well. Each family has its own private entrance, small porch, tiny kitchen, single bedroom and bathroom, and living room area. Shelly and Shoshana have no telephone. Little cooking is done in the Lilker home since the kibbutz provides all meals in a modern community dining hall. The private kitchen is for home entertaining and family snacks. Younger kibbutz children study at a local elementary school encompassing six kibbutzim, and older students attend a regional high school in a neighboring community. Shoshana as the kibbutz librarian and Shelly as the general secretary have full-time jobs, as do all the kibbutz members.

K'far Ha-Macabi is run as a participatory direct democracy with each member having an equal share and vote in the community's policies and decisions. General town meetings are convened at least twice a month to decide critical issues related to education, housing, work, kibbutz finances, health care, leisure activities, culture, and new construction. The general meeting also approves the candidacy of new members usually following a trial period of one year.

The kibbutz uses no money in its internal dealings and goods are distributed according to each member's need. There are no privately owned cars on the kibbutz; instead, K'far Ha-Macabi members may use kibbutz vehicles for their personal use. Members are given special allowances for clothing, travel, furniture, hobbies, and even cigarettes. The kibbutz provides each of its members with total health care from womb to tomb. Food and shelter are also provided. With the kibbutz's approval, members can take a leave of absence to attend a college or university or to take training courses to develop special skills like animal husbandry, computer science, or nutritional expertise—skills that will benefit the kibbutz. Such educational projects do not affect the financial security of the member's family. The kibbutz kitchen, dining hall, orchards, fields, barns, chicken coops, ponds, laundry, library, factories, and business office are all staffed by kibbutz members. In recent years some kibbutzim have expanded their economic base and have been forced to hire outside labor to maintain productivity. The nonkibbutz workers receive salaries just as they would at any other place of work. In addition, when kibbutz members are employed outside the kibbutz in various capacities that offer greater professional opportunities than can be found in the kibbutz itself, they continue to live on their home kibbutz and participate fully in its life. Their outside salaries are contributed to the kibbutz. This was the procedure that Shelly Lilker followed while he was on the Technion's faculty.

Often the jobs are rotated among the kibbutz members. But sometimes, as in Shoshana's case, permanent duties match one's professional training. Every fourth Shabbat, Shelly takes his turn washing dishes in the K'far Ha-Macabi community kitchen. Over the years, all four members of the Lilker family have performed many varied tasks of the kibbutz. Tami is especially interested in environmental protection and intends to pursue this interest upon completion of her army duty.

In its early years the kibbutzim were exclusively engaged in agriculture. This reflected practical considerations as well as an ideological commitment. Because of extraordinary innovations and research in this area, the kibbutzim have achieved an internationally recognized standard of excellence in developing new and successful agricultural methods, especially in raising crops with little water and in barren soil.

In recent years many kibbutzim have branched out into industrial production. This has occurred as kibbutz members have grown older and can no longer maintain the vigorous schedule of physical labor of earlier years. Diversification also became necessary once Israel achieved total self-sufficiency in feeding its population. K'far Ha-Macabi still produces thousands of chickens, millions of eggs, and tons of vegetables as cash crops along with fish from the kibbutz's freshwater ponds. It also maintains a herd of dairy cows. But the kibbutz has also undertaken a new commercial venture—the recapping of used rubber tires. The recycled tires are exported to Western Europe for sale. Like its sister kibbutzim, K'far Ha-Macabi still maintains its traditional collective structure and life style, but it has clearly moved into the highly competitive world of international trade and commerce. Shelly is confident his kibbutz will be successful in this new economic venture. "We are building a new infrastructure at K'far Ha-Macabi, really building for the future, for our children."

Kibbutz children have participated in a unique seventy-year-long experiment in child rearing. One of the most radical innovations of kibbutz living has been the rearing of young boys and girls away from the parents' homes. Some kibbutzim follow the strict policy of placing all children, including infants, in a community *bayt yeladim* (children's house) where they are raised outside of the parental home through adolescence. Of course, in all cases children and parents live on the same kibbutz and spend many hours together. The objective is to free the parents, especially mothers, from their classic role as twenty-four-hour guardians of their children. The kibbutz provides a total day-and-night-care-center program that allows parents to pursue their professional kibbutz tasks. It is also believed that such kibbutz children will become mature, self-reliant, and psychologically healthy adults.

K'far Ha-Macabi has modified this classic child-rearing program. Boys and girls live with their parents until age thirteen. They then move to a bayt yeladim, in effect, creating a second home on the same kibbutz. Some child-rearing experts maintain that this procedure provides a healthy alternative to living with one's parents during the turbulent teen-age years. Other experts, however, disagree, claiming that children who are deprived of continuous parental companionship often become emotionally cold and aloof. After seventy years and three generations of children, the question remains unresolved.

Shoshana questions the quality of life the bayt yeladim has provided for Tami and Ari. She wonders what the effects of having two separate homes will be upon her children. "With Shelly and me they are part of a nuclear family within the kibbutz, but at the bayt yeladim they live with their peers in a close-knit youth community . . . a different set of values and standards. I wonder which is better?"

In the summer of 1981, Tami began her compulsory two-year army service. All eighteen-year-old Israeli men and women are drafted into the military. Only a few exemptions are granted, usually to married women or to extremely Orthodox young people. Ari, a year younger than his sister, will also serve in the Israeli army when he becomes eighteen. Thus, college and university educations do not usually begin for Israelis until they have completed their required military service.

This has meant an older and usually more mature student body on Israel's campuses. Women remain in the military reserves until they marry or until they reach the age of twenty-four, if they remain single. Men continue in the reserves until age fifty-five. The reserve program is a demanding one with four weeks annually set aside for intensive training as well as regular military duty. This reserve duty, so necessary for Israel's defense, is a negative factor in the nation's economic development. To have so many people away from their normal jobs hinders economic growth and disrupts personal lives and careers. However, Israel depends upon its citizen army for national defense, and the reserve units are indispensable. Israel's standing army is quite small, so its well-trained reserves must be ready for rapid mobilization, an ability that was evident in the 1967 and 1973 Arab-Israeli wars.

Why did Shelly and Shoshana Lilker choose the kibbutz style of life for themselves and their two children? How successfully have they adjusted to collective living? The Lilkers chose the kibbutz because it offered a "total immersion into a Hebrew-speaking Jewish community," a community that is unpretentious and unadorned. Unlike some other kibbutzim, K'far Ha-Macabi does not operate a guesthouse for tourists and other visitors. All of the kibbutz's facilities are highly functional, simple, and are solely for the use of K'far Ha-Macabi's members.

"As a kid growing up in the United States, I was never very interested in acquiring personal goods and money. I didn't think they were evil or corrupting, I just never devoted much energy to it. Ironically, today I'm extremely involved in the total financial structure of our kibbutz . . . such things as cash flow, profits, productivity, marketing, and maintenance of facilities and equipment. Now it's not an individual thing, not what Shelly Lilker can acquire, but rather what can keep K'far Ha-Macabi and its members financially solvent . . . something very different."

Will Tami and Ari return to the kibbutz after army duty and college? "Neither Shelly nor I can predict what our children will do. Can any parent? Many kibbutz children do come back, but there's no coercion to join a kibbutz, no active recruitment. It's a voluntary thing but, of course, once you do join K'far Ha-Macabi you must live in accordance with our kibbutz's policies and practices. No matter what Tami and Ari do, Shelly and I will remain on the kibbutz," Shoshana said.

I asked Shelly and Shoshana if they have found fulfillment on K'far Ha-Macabi. "Fulfillment," he laughed. "What's that? But yes, I think I have found it. The kibbutz is my kind of Jewish living, on the land, speaking Hebrew, being productive in Israel. The kibbutz is not for every Jew, nor for every Israeli, but it's for me. Being the 'mazkir' is a little like being a congregational rabbi back in the States. Despite the utopian vision of the kibbutz, every kind of interpersonal conflict exists here like anywhere else. I'm often bombarded with personal complaints and problems. The economic pressures on K'far Ha-Macabi are getting more acute. We've had to diversify and be concerned about our aging members. Our kibbutz is over forty years old, but we'll continue to make it."

Shelly grew pensive and said, "We have made it since K'far Ha-Macabi was founded in 1936. We support ourselves; each of us has experienced our own Jewish rebirth here. We've raised our children, and we've trained others to start their own kibbutzim. The Reform Jewish movement in the States has recently established kibbutz Yahel in the Negev wilderness, north of Eilat. We trained the founding cadre of Yahel. As a Reform rabbi, I'm especially proud of that."

Do the Lilkers ever feel isolated or confined to their little kibbutz of three hundred fifty men, women, and children? "Of course not. After all, we're not prisoners here: We have radio and TV and, of course, there is a good library. And Haifa is only twenty-five minutes away by car. Besides, the kibbutz provides cultural programs. It has all the cultural life we need," Shelly answered.

As one K'far Ha-Macabi member put it: "Our kibbutz is the real thing . . . no tourists, many, many sabras, plain functional buildings, and lots of hard work." But it is also not an austere Spartan retreat center cut off from the world, nor is it filled with physical or psychological hermits. With its modern and spacious dining hall, an attractive snack bar and lounge area, lovely flowers and shrubbery, an excellent library and an inviting swimming pool, K'far Ha-Macabi is an attractive place to live.

"When we became kibbutz members we did not leave the human race or Israeli society. We are very much a part of both," Shelly said. His doctoral thesis deals with Jewish religious observances and practices on kibbutzim. He discovered that the kibbutz movement has adapted and recast many traditions of Diaspora Judaism to meet the needs of the kibbutzniks who are at home on the land of Israel. "Kibbutz members ask the same questions as anyone else, but they've reshaped religious practices to blend in with our agricultural way of life. Kibbutzniks are very pragmatic and not too interested in theological speculation; but one thing is sure: the social values of the kibbutz and its way of life have encouraged kibbutz members to lead a life that is distinguished by helpfulness and mutual cooperation. I think these are religious qualities and we have them on a kibbutz."

Shalom Lilker concluded his thesis with these words: "Although the self-critical stance of the kibbutz plays a healthy role, it could get out of hand without the balance afforded by the celebration of living and of the kibbutz way of life that is possible only through the joyous observance of the holidays and festivals of the Jewish people." Clearly, he has not ceased being a rabbi; it's just that his "congregation" is different.

Katya and Eli Azoulay represent a different kind of Israeli life style. They are in their early thirties and have two young sons—Gabi, who was born in 1974, and Ron, who is two years younger. They live in a small, but well furnished, two-bedroom apartment in Neve Yaakov about eight miles north of central Jerusalem. Neve Yaakov is a cluster of high rise buildings that were constructed after the 1967 Six-Day War. In 1925 the Neve Yaakov kibbutz was established; it was attacked by the Arabs during the anti-Jewish riots of 1929. The original kibbutz was overrun in the 1948 war and had to be abandoned by its residents.

Following the reunification of Jerusalem in 1967, the area of the original kibbutz was incorporated into the city limits of Israel's capital. Neve Yaakov experienced a rebirth, this time as a suburban apartment development for hundreds of young Jewish families, including the Azoulays.

Like Shoshana Lilker, Eli Azoulay was also born in Jerusalem. Eli's parents were members of the ancient Jewish community of Fez, Morocco; but with nearly seven hundred fifty thousand other Jews from Arab countries, they emigrated to Israel after the Jewish state gained independence in 1948. Eli has six sisters and brothers, all of whom still live in Jerusalem, and his parents have thirteen sabra grandchildren.

Eli's huge family is important to him, and was the focal point of his childhood years. "I have so many aunts and uncles and cousins. Moroccan Jews are especially close to each other. Perhaps in a couple of generations that may change, but right now, we are all close to one another," Eli said.

A graduate of the Hadassah Community College in Jerusalem, Eli is currently a computer systems analyst with the Ministry of Trade and Commerce. He commutes daily to his Jerusalem office by public bus since the Azoulays do not own a car.

Eli's family life and professional career are interrupted each year by four weeks of army duty. He was wounded in 1969 during the Egyptian-Israeli War of Attrition at the Suez Canal, and Eli also served during the 1973 Yom Kippur War. Like other Israeli men, Eli must remain in the active reserves until he is fifty-five years old. "The army is the army. What can I say? I have to serve, and, after all, if I don't do it, who will? Maybe my sons won't have to go into the army, maybe, but I doubt it," he said.

His wife, Katya, was born in New York City where she received her elementary and high school education. She graduated from Brearley, a small fashionable Manhattan girls' school. When she was twenty years old she went to Hebrew University to study and remained as an *olah*, a new immigrant to Israel. Her Viennese-born mother had fled the Nazis with her family, coming to the United States as a child in 1938. Katya's black father was born in Jamaica and emigrated to the U.S. when he was twelve.

"I was raised with Jewish values, black consciousness, and taught that as a black Jewish woman I must always strive to achieve a world of equality and humanity. I visited both Jamaica and Israel, and chose to live in Israel because I felt I could best serve my roots there as a black Jewish woman," Katya remarked. "I had come to Israel on a visit in 1966 and was taken with Israel and its spirit, and returned to stay in 1970. Two years later, I met Eli," she recounted. In 1973 they were married in the historic Rabbi Yohanan ben Zakkai Synagogue in the Old City of Jerusalem. That ancient Sephardic house of worship had been destroyed during the Jordanian occupation of the city, but it was reconstructed after the 1967 war. "We were one of the first couples to be married in the rebuilt synagogue," Katya said.

Following their wedding, the Azoulays lived in a small apartment in Jerusalem that was owned by the Hebrew University, where Katya was enrolled as a student. The births of their two sons and the financial demands of a growing family interrupted Katya's education. They moved from Jerusalem and lived for two years in the southern Israeli port city of Eilat. Eli was a youth counselor and, although the Azoulays loved the desert climate and the pioneering spirit of Eilat, they both yearned to return to Jerusalem. "It's a special place. I love it and don't want to live anywhere else. After all, I was born in Jerusalem, it's my home," Eli said. In 1977 they returned to Israel's capital city.

Eli and Katya rent their Neve Yaakov apartment, a rarity in Israel where most apartments (or "flats" as they are called) are usually co-ops or condominiums. Neve Yaakov's buildings are filled with hundreds of young Israeli families, thousands of youngsters, and many pregnant women. The community's population is eighteen thousand. But surprisingly the community does not have adequate day-care facilities for the children of working parents. Neve Yaakov has no movie theater or swimming pool for its residents. Its synagogue, however, is quite active with many programs. "Our community recreation program is poor, but we hope for some government action soon," Katya remarked.

The roof of the Azoulays' apartment house affords a magnificent view of Jerusalem from the north. Mount Scopus, with its rebuilt Hebrew University campus and the Hadassah Medical Center, is clearly visible along with the bleak Judean wilderness. While the area was under Jordanian control, King Hussein began construction of a summer royal palace, an escape from the desert heat of the capital in Amman. Hussein's military defeat in 1967 prevented him from completing the project, but the shell of the palace which can be seen from Neve Yaakov is a graphic reminder of recent Middle East history.

Eli and Katya do not believe that Israel will ever give up Neve Yaakov in any future peace negotiations. "Neve Yaakov is part of Jerusalem, it's not the West Bank, and Jerusalem will never be redivided again," Eli asserted. "People often forget that the first Jewish settlement here was the kibbutz nearly sixty years ago."

Katya has resumed her Hebrew University studies, majoring in African studies. "Israel desperately needs to relate to Africa in a positive way. So few Israelis know or care about Africa, especially after many black African states broke off relations with Israel after the 1973 war. Israelis generally focus on the Middle East, with great emphasis on Europe and North America, but Africa is so close to us and so important," Katya declared. After completing her academic work, she hopes to make a contribution to improving Israeli–black-African relations, perhaps working for the Foreign Ministry.

Katya Azoulay has obviously given up much to live in Israel. She and her sabra sons are nearly six thousand miles away from her parents who live in New York City. Infrequent visits to the U.S. do not make up for the long distance between grandparents and grandsons. Katya has also sacrificed many creature comforts as well, including a car and a house, but Israel has given her something very precious in return. What that something is came out in a Sabbath dinner conversation in her apartment.

Although she takes enormous pride in Israel's many achievements, Katya and her husband worry that some Israelis "have forgotten the real purpose of the state—a just and progressive Jewish society, a place to live a fully Jewish life as the majority population in our own land." Her fulfillment (the "something") comes as she and her husband strive to live out their aspirations and dreams for Israel.

K'far Ha-Macabi and Neve Yaakov rarely appear on a tourist's basic itinerary. Few, if any, tourist buses stop at either community, and neither is among the "must see" attractions for foreign visitors of the Jewish state. These places do not appear in the many beautiful picture books about Israel that have been published, and the two communities do not even rate a post card! Yet K'far Ha-Macabi and Neve Yaakov are both vital parts of an Israel that is unadorned for visitors and unself-conscious. They are part of the Israel that exists behind the newspaper headlines and the nightly TV news programs that so decisively shape what most Americans learn and know about the Jewish state.

It is precisely at places like K'far Ha-Macabi and Neve Yaakov, seemingly so different in setting and life style from each other, that the future of Israel will be determined. One community is a forty-five-year-old kibbutz near Haifa that offers a distinctive kind of Israeli life, providing a close-knit collective community structure that apparently meets the physical and psychological needs of its members. Neve Yaakov, however, is a new and vast apartment house complex that is filled with many young families, all striving to succeed in an inflationary Israeli society. It lacks the community facilities and unique life style of the kibbutz, but Neve Yaakov has a vitality of its own. Some of the Azoulays' neighbors and friends are Jews from Kurdistan, Turkey and the United States, while many are, of course, like Eli, native-born sabras. The eighteen thousand residents reflect the reality of the sometimes abstract concept, "the ingathering of the exiles," since they have come from almost every country of the Jewish Diaspora to live in Israel.

Why did Shelly Lilker (the rabbi) and Katya Azoulay (the university student) move to Israel from the United States? Their answers are remarkably similar: to lead a full and free Jewish life in the ancient homeland. Both married Jerusalem-born sabras and are currently raising their children in a Jewish environment that is far different from their own childhoods in the Diaspora.

The two families raise important questions about modern Israeli society. Can K'far Ha-Macabi and other kibbutzim successfully move from a basically agricultural economy to a new and more diversified industrial base? Can such a change take place without severely disrupting the kibbutz's original purpose and philosophy? Can Israel fulfill the upward socio-economic aspirations of the Azoulays and the other young couples of Neve Yaakov? Can Eli and Katya move to more responsible and better paying positions? The crucial litmus test for Israel will be how successfully it absorbs the four Lilker and Azoulay children into its society. Will there be adequate housing, quality education, and meaningful employment for Tami, Ari, Gaby, and Ron? Israel's future development depends on positive answers to these questions.

Every developing society in the world today faces similar challenges, but Israel was founded with extremely high hopes, goals, and expectations: a progressive and egalitarian society living in peace with its Arab neighbors, a society that provides its citizens with unlimited opportunities for personal and national fulfillment as Jews. It is not an overstatement to say: as go the Lilkers and the Azoulays, so goes Israel.

7 | *Israel and the Christian Community*

The last eight years of Theodor Herzl's life (1896–1904) were frenzied ones as he desperately sought to secure a Jewish state legally. In early 1904, a few months before his death, Herzl met with Pope Pius X at the Vatican. It was a dramatic scene; nothing like it had ever happened before. The world leader of the Roman Catholic church met with the world leader of the Zionist movement to discuss the possibility of a reborn Jewish state in the Holy Land—the land of the biblical patriarchs and matriarchs, the Prophets, and Jesus.

Herzl was hopeful that he could obtain the "good will of the Holy See" for the Zionist program. But Herzl's hopes were dashed when Pius X responded negatively to the Zionist leader's request for Vatican understanding and support. The pope's statement was a clear articulation of one kind of Christian attitude toward Jews, Judaism, and Zionism: "We cannot approve of the Zionist movement. We cannot prevent the Hebrews from going to Jerusalem, but we could never sanction it. The Hebrews have not recognized our Lord, therefore, we cannot recognize the Hebrew people. . . . " Herzl described for the pope the terrible suffering of the Jews who lived in the anti-Semitic countries of Europe, only to hear the reply: "If you come to Palestine and settle your people there, we shall keep churches and priests ready to baptize all of them."

The pope's rejection of the Zionist endeavor left Herzl in a depressed mood. However, two weeks later, Cardinal Merry del Val, the papal secretary of state, softened the Vatican's position when he told one of Herzl's aides: "If the Jews believe they might greatly ease their lot by being admitted to the land of their ancestors, then we would regard that as a humanitarian question. We shall never forget that without Judaism, we would have been nothing." The two statements, one by the pope and the other by a cardinal, graphically illustrate the ambivalence and ambiguity that have often character-ized Christian reactions to Zionism and to its creation, the state of Israel. Herzl's meeting with Pius X provided one of the first official Christian responses to the issue, but it was not to be the last.

Indeed, the return of the Jews to Eretz Israel and the emergence of the state of Israel have presented Christianity with several pro-found questions: If the Jews are condemned and punished by God to be perpetual wanderers in the world, a people eternally in exile because they did not accept Jesus as the Messiah, then what does the rebirth of an independent Jewish state mean for Christian theology? Does Israel have any theological significance for Christianity? Is the creation of Israel one of God's signs in history, or is it a totally human event, free of all religious meaning? What role, if any, should theology play in shaping Christian attitudes toward Israel?

Historically, there have been three major distinctive Christian responses to Israel, and each response has evoked fervent support as well as bitter opposition from Christians throughout the world. These three schools of thought do not exhaust the range of Christian reactions, but they do represent some basic trends within the churches of the world.

One Christian response is rooted in the many biblical verses that speak of a Jewish restoration in the land of Israel. One of the first Christians to expound this view in the 1890s was the Protestant chap-lain at the British Embassy in Vienna, William Hechler. Like many other British Christians, Hechler saw Zionism as a "biblically pro-phetic" movement that would reestablish a Jewish state "just as in the days of David and Solomon." The Christian chaplain was at-tracted to Herzl, and he helped the Zionist leader obtain some meet-ings with several important European political figures. Hechler be-came a passionate Christian Zionist whose philo-Semitism reflected a powerful stream within Christian religious thought: the ingather-ing of the Jewish people to the Holy Land and the creation of a Jew-ish commonwealth are essential preconditions for the Second Com-ing of Jesus the Christ. The Jewish state is a necessary component of Christian theology, a fulfillment of prophecy.

For such Christians, Israel is God's chosen people (Deut. 7:6–8), the state of Israel is a fulfillment of prophecy (Isa. 43:5–6; Ezekiel 37), Israel occupies a special place in God's kingdom (Ezek. 36:30, 33–38; Amos 9:1–15; Zech. 8:22–23; Romans 9–11), and Israel has a God-ordained right to the land (Deuteronomy 28—30; Acts 7:5).

Millions of Christians, both clergy and lay, share this belief. Most are within the evangelical branch of Christianity. The prominent evangelist, Billy Graham, and a host of other Christian leaders, including Arnold T. Olson, a former president of the Evangelical Free Church of America, have been strong public supporters of Israel. Carl Edwin Armerding, a leading evangelical biblical scholar, has written:

> I believe we need an evangelical community that recognizes its debt to Israel and sees the modern state of Israel as an important part of the very existence of God's ancient people. . . . It [the evangelical community] can and should actively consider the political and economic needs of modern Israel, if for no other reason than that Israel is an expression of a people beloved by God.

A second major Christian response to Israel is also highly supportive, but it is not directly linked to biblical prophecy or eschatology. This position is primarily based on the twin concepts of justice and morality for the Jewish people. According to this position, the Jews have been brutally victimized by Christians and Christianity in every part of the world for nearly twenty centuries. The Holocaust took place in Europe and was carried out by men and women who were baptized Christians—including Hitler, Himmler, and Goering. That unspeakable horror is viewed as the culmination of centuries of negative Christian teachings and practices toward Jews and Judaism.

This second response or position argues that the creation of the state of Israel can in no way atone for past Christian sins against the Jewish people, nor can it wipe the slate of history clean for Christianity. Solidarity with Israel, however, is one concrete and compassionate way to begin the Christian process of eradicating anti-Semitism and of building a healthy and respectful relationship with the Jewish people who have been wronged by Christians for so long.

The existence of a secure Jewish state represents the Jewish people's collective right to self-determination and national identity. Until his death in 1971, Reinhold Niebuhr was the acknowledged leader of Christians who support Israel for moral and juridical reasons. Today

Niebuhr's disciples are found in many American churches and religious organizations as well as on Christian seminary and university faculties. Niebuhr advocated a "Christian realism" toward Zionism and Israel, a doctrine that did not negate the biblical promises but focused instead on the compelling and devastating existential realities of the Jewish people in the twentieth century.

Foremost among Niebuhr's many spiritual heirs are Protestants Franklin H. Littell of Temple University, Roy and Alice Eckardt of Lehigh University, and Roman Catholics John Pawlikowski of Catholic Theological Union, Eugene Fisher, the executive secretary of the U.S. Bishops' Secretariat for Catholic-Jewish Relations, and Edward H. Flannery, the first executive secretary for Catholic-Jewish Relations, who currently teaches at Our Lady of Providence Seminary in Rhode Island. Father Flannery has written:

> In view of the ceaseless persecutions visited upon Jews so often by Christians throughout the centuries, and because of their scattered state throughout the world, it is the Christian, above all, who should rejoice at the upturn in the Jewish people's fortunes in our time that has brought them back to their ancient homeland. The return to Israel can only be seen as the righting of a historical wrong.

The third major Christian response to Israel has been highly negative and critical. It is a blending of two streams of Christian thought that has created an intense anti-Zionism that questions the very right of Israel to exist as a sovereign state. For well over a century, American Christian groups, especially Protestant churches, have maintained an active missionary presence in the Arab Middle East. Since the end of World War II and with the emergence of many independent Arab states, the Christian effort has stressed humanitarian concerns like schools, universities, orphanages, clinics, and hospitals. Not surprisingly, some American Christians who served in the Arab Middle East became "more Arab than the Arabs" in their attitudes toward Israel. They have often taken more extreme anti-Israel positions than their Arab hosts. In 1974 the National Council of Churches–American Jewish Committee interreligious delegation met with Western Christian representatives who were based in Jordan. A relief specialist from a large Protestant denomination told his Christian and Jewish listeners in Amman that "Israel's behavior will fan anti-Semitism throughout the world . . . and will increase the precarious situation of Jews in the world." He was sharply criticized by the visiting Christians and Jews who felt he was making the victims of anti-Semitism responsible for their own victimization. The Christian Middle East representative admitted he "expected more from Israel than from the Arabs since, after all, the Jews really do not have the right to the land."

Some of the Christian missionaries to the Arab world have returned to the U.S. and assumed important leadership positions within their denominations. They often serve in the foreign divisions or the overseas ministries of their church bodies. Such missionaries usually bring with them the anti-Israel attitudes they either developed or inherited while in the Arab states.

Some of these missionaries, however, have never been in Israel even though they spent many years in the Middle East. Nor have some of them had much direct contact with the Jewish community in the United States. Thus, their basic animus to Israel is sometimes combined with an ignorance of the Jewish state and of the Jewish community in the Diaspora. This has resulted in highly negative anti-Israel policies and actions on the part of some American Protestant church bodies.

This third Christian response to Israel attempts to remove or vitiate all of the biblical promises made to the Jewish people. Some Christian theologians and Bible scholars have long taught that ancient Israel, the "old Israel" of the "old covenant" has been replaced by the "new Israel" of the "new covenant," the Christian church. Israel's spiritual vocation and mission has thus been transferred from the Jewish people to the church. The Jews are left out in the theological cold, a people without a *raison d'être* or purpose. Not only has such Christian thinking rendered the Jews vulnerable to violent anti-Semitism, it has also negated any Jewish claim to the land of Israel because it maintains such claims have been emptied of all concrete meaning. Those claims have either been fulfilled by Christianity or "spiritualized" into an abstraction devoid of flesh-and-blood reality. Hence, any attempt by the Jewish people to regain national sovereignty and independence, indeed, any link to the biblical promises, are no longer valid. All Jewish claims have been superceded by Judaism's rightful successor, Christianity. This concept of "theological displacement" is held by many Christians, especially those from Middle Eastern churches. Some Western Christians share this view as well. In 1977, the patriarch of the Syrian-based Antiochian Orthodox Church, Elias IV, visited the United States. At a news conference in Washington he declared that Jews had little "historic connection" with the territory of the state of Israel. Speaking through his interpreter, Elias said, "As far as we Christians are concerned, we are the new Israel. All the prophecies of the Old Testament were fulfilled by the coming of the Messiah. . . . After the destruction of the Temple, the Jews were dispersed. Those who remained lived in peace with the Arabs and the Christians" until modern times when, he said, "outsiders" came into the land.

The clear intention of such a position is to theologically delegitimize the Jewish state and to deny it any authentic linkage with the biblical promises of land and peoplehood. If Israel's biblical roots can be permanently severed, then the Jewish state, like the Jewish people, becomes a theological "artificial entity" similar to the political illegitimacy Israel has been accorded in the Palestinian National Covenant.

This position has resulted in theological anti-Semitism on the part of some Christian leaders. In 1980, the National Council of Churches, which represents thirty-one American Protestant and Orthodox denominations, sent a "blue ribbon" leadership group to several Arab countries and Israel to gather firsthand information for a proposed Middle East policy statement. In its contacts with Arab Christians, the NCC panel encountered a theological anti-Jewish bias. The NCC group sadly noted this fact in its report. Despite the carefully guarded language, the discomfort of the American Christians is clear:

> In the contacts the panel had with some Middle East Christians, it was reminded of the theological differences that still exist within the Christian community over the meaning of the Abrahamic covenant and the continuing role of the Jewish people. Most panel members saw that some theological positions, when combined with the political dynamics of the area could be understood as what the West would call anti-Semitism. Thus, the seeds of religious alienation can be carried through the churches themselves. . . .

In any serious discussion of Israel, four central issues are often raised by Christians to help them gain greater insight and knowledge. First, it is especially difficult for many Christians, even those who are supportive of Israel, to grasp the inextricable bond between the Jewish people and the land of Israel. In the 1930s and 1940s, this question enlivened the editorial pages of the *Christian Century*, a leading journal of Protestant opinion. Even in the darkest days of the Holocaust, the *Christian Century* maintained a consistent anti-Zionist position. In 1939, the magazine carried an article by Daniel Bliss, a prominent American missionary to the Middle East: "There is plenty of room for nonpolitical Jews (those who did not advocate Jewish nationalism) in Palestine. . . . " It was Britain's "solemn duty to protect and safeguard the *permanent Jewish minority* [emphasis added]." In 1933 the magazine editorially urged American Jews to bring pressure on Nazi leaders so that Jews could continue to live in Germany rather than embark on the "chimerical scheme" of emigrating to Palestine.

In 1964, under the leadership of its new editor, Kyle Haseldon, the *Century* shifted its policy toward Israel, becoming more positive. The current editor, James Wall, is supportive of Israel, while still reserving the right to criticize a specific Israeli action or policy. Since the 1940s there have been much greater Christian understanding and appreciation of the Jewish link to the land of Israel. The past three decades have witnessed a remarkable growth of Christian-Jewish dialogues in North America and Western Europe. Since the Six-Day War of 1967, both Jews and Christians have made Israel a central part of such conversations. Positive teaching material about Israel has been introduced into many Christian schools and seminaries, but much more work needs to be done in this area to correct the theological and political anti-Israel bias so often found in Christian education.

An authoritative Christian response to the question of the land and the Jewish people has come from the World Council of Churches, an international body of over three hundred Protestant and Orthodox churches. In 1982 the WCC's Executive Committee approved the Guidelines for Jewish-Christian Dialogue that were drafted by the Council's Consultation on the Church and the Jewish People. The WCC Guidelines declared:

> There was no time in which the memory of the land of Israel and of Zion, the city of Jerusalem, was not central in the worship and hope of the Jewish people. "Next year in Jerusalem" was always part

of Jewish worship in the Diaspora. And the continuing presence of Jews in the Land and in Jerusalem was always more than just one place of residence among all the others.

Jews differ in their interpretations of the state of Israel, as to its religious and secular meaning. It constitutes for them part of the long search for that survival which has always been central to Judaism through the ages. . . .

The second question that Christians ask centers on the nature and necessity of a Jewish state. They wonder whether Israel is a theocracy with Judaism as the official state religion. Christians also ask whether a Jewish state is really needed for the Jewish people's self-fulfillment.

Although Judaism is the religion of the overwhelming majority of the country's citizens, it is not the established state religion. As indicated earlier, an important debate is going on within Israel regarding the role of Judaism in the society. Nor is Israel a theocracy. Christianity in its many expressions, both Eastern and Western, and the religion of Islam are accorded full freedom. Churches and mosques abound, religious education is widespread, and the holy places are open and administered by the appropriate religious authorities. The Jewish people did not return to their homeland to create a state that would impose its religious will upon non-Jews.

Israel is in a region of the world that is filled with Islamic extremism and with Arab states that have made Islam the state religion. Yet Israel remains a nation of religious diversity and pluralism.

A Jewish state can be best understood as the "state of the Jewish people"—the one country in the world whose national life is shaped by unique Jewish values based on historic and religious experience. The Jewish state is the one place where Jews as the majority in their own land can mold their culture, education, politics, economics, and religion.

A cruel history has taught the Jewish people that the goal of determining one's national destiny can only be achieved in a state of their own. A Jewish state is the one country that will always admit a Jew—the one place a Jew can go when all other ports of refuge and safety are closed, as they have often been in the long course of Jewish history. Israel's national purpose is to welcome every Jew who wants to live there. That is why the Israeli Law of Return provides each entering Jew with immediate Israeli citizenship. After centuries of expulsion, forced religious conversions, pogroms, second-class citizenship and/or no citizenship rights, and genocide, Jews are entitled to a compensatory affirmative action policy of instant citizenship. Christians and Muslims who emigrate to Israel can also become citizens, but their progress is a formal naturalization process similar to the American model.

Critics of Zionism have argued since Herzl's time that self-fulfillment for the Jewish people is best achieved by remaining a creative minority within the larger societies and nations of the world. However, this position, even when it is eloquently argued, must confront the grim historical results of nearly two thousand years of Jewish statelessness.

Adin Steinsaltz, a leading rabbi in Israel, has spoken of the necessity of a Jewish state in this way: "Judaism without a state is like a person without a body. . . . Judaism cannot be fulfilled only in the synagogue. First, we are a community, then we are a city [Jerusalem], and then we must be a state." The National Council of Churches in its Middle East Policy Statement recognized this fact when it demanded that the PLO, as a step to peace, revise the Palestinian National Covenant in order to recognize "Israel as a sovereign state and its right to continue as a Jewish state."

A third question that is often asked by Christians deals with the relationship between Zionism and Judaism. Are they linked together? Is it possible to separate Zionism from Judaism? Some critics of Israel have attempted to do just that—defining Zionism as a narrow, parochial, and even racist form of nationalism as opposed to the universal Jewish religion. This exercise creates a distorted and schizophrenic view of reality since the religion cannot be divorced from the flesh-and-blood reality of the Jewish people who have made Zionism, the national liberation movement, into one of the foundations of their collective faith commitment.

Zionism is not a modern nationalism artificially placed upon an ancient people and religion. Rather, it is an amalgam of the ancient with the modern, the religious with the secular, the theological with the historic. Zionism is an integral part of the Jewish religion.

Adherents of such a false dichotomy usually declare that one can be "anti-Zionist" without being "anti-Semitic." By this they mean there can be sharp criticism of Zionism, while at the same time remaining free of anti-Semitic feelings and attitudes. In effect, they assert that one may even question the very existence of the Zionist creation, the Jewish state, without being anti-Jewish. It is a position that cannot be honestly maintained.

It is always necessary to look closely at the motivations of the person or group who claims to be merely anti-Zionist and not anti-Semitic. The harshest critics of ancient Israel were the Hebrew prophets, and so too today some of the most severe critics of Israel come quite naturally from the Israeli Jews themselves, an obvious sign of the nation's health and democratic character. But in both cases the chastisements were given *b'ahavah*, in a spirit of love and support for the erring people and nation. Neither the prophets nor today's Israelis advocate the end or destruction of the Jewish state. Their critiques were and are delivered with the hope of national self-correction and improvement.

This is not so in the case of many self-proclaimed anti-Zionists. Their ultimate goal in criticizing the flaws of modern Israel and Zionism is not to change Israeli behavior but to destroy the Jewish state itself.

One can certainly criticize specific actions of Israel. Every state is imperfect in some of its policies and actions, and Israel is no exception to this sad but true fact of national life. But criticism of Israeli actions is far different than an attack on the movement that brought Israel into being. Anti-Zionism is a three-pronged assault on the continued existence of the Jewish state, on the people who live in that state, and upon the Jews of other countries who support Israel.

The clearest example of this campaign to discredit Zionism while allegedly remaining free of anti-Semitism was the 1975 United Nations General Assembly resolution that called Zionism "a form of racism and racial discrimination." The overwhelming Christian reaction to the UN vote was immediate and almost uniformly critical of the resolution. World Christian leaders, pastors, educators, and lay people were not fooled by the Arab- and Soviet-backed resolution. Christians clearly saw the direct connection between the anti-Zionism of the UN action and the danger of anti-Semitism. Claire Randall, the NCC's general secretary, spoke out against the resolution and charged that it "has the potential for reviving an old form of racism, anti-Semitism, in many places of the world." Philip Potter, the WCC's general secretary, urged the UN to "reconsider and rescind" its action, and he rejected the definition of Zionism as racist. For Potter, Zionism is a "complex historical process expressing many differing aspirations of the Jewish people over the years, and . . . subject to many misunderstandings and interpretations. None of these could appropriately be used to condemn Zionism as racism."

Archbishop Iakovos, primate of the Greek Orthodox Church in North and South America, called the resolution "deplorable and offensive." Archbishop Joseph L. Bernardin, then president of the United States Catholic Conference, asserted that the UN action "opens the door to harassment, discrimination and denial of basic rights to members of the Jewish community throughout the world."

The fourth question that many Christians ask focuses on the relationship between Israel and the Diaspora. Some early Zionist leaders negated the Diaspora, calling it a two-thousand-year-old abnormality, an exile that must be ended to restore national independence to the Jewish people. They maintained that the presence of communities outside of Israel for two millenniums did not, however, justify the Diaspora's continued existence. The rebirth of Israel signaled the end of Jewish minority status in the rest of the world. Such thinkers assert that the Diaspora has produced a truncated and basically unhealthy Jewish people who are the vulnerable minority everywhere without the power to shape their own lives. The Zionist movement says to every Jew who lives outside of Israel: come home at last!

Other thinkers, however, accept the Diaspora as an authentic form of Jewish life. They cite the many extraordinary achievements of the *Golah*, the Hebrew term for the Diaspora. These include the Babylonian Talmud; the significant religious writings of Moses Maimonides, Moses Mendelssohn, Abraham Joshua Heschel and others; the rise of the Hasidic movement as well as the Orthodox, Conservative, Reconstructionist, and Reform expressions of Judaism; and the development of Jewish mysticism, poetry, art, music, liturgy, and law as Jews came into contact with many diverse peoples and cultures in all parts of the world. The Golah, far from being a negative factor, actually maintained and enriched Jewish life during the long centuries when there was no Jewish state.

In addition, the creation of the state of Israel has not brought the Diaspora to an end. Most of the world's Jews, about 10 million, still live in the Golah while 3.3 million are in Israel. Many of those 10 million reside in the free countries of North America, Western Europe, and Australia. Unless there is a major political upheaval in those lands, the Diaspora is likely to continue.

Many Jews hold a "both/and" approach that affirms the necessity and centrality of a free and secure Israel, while still recognizing the importance and authenticity of the Diaspora. The traumatic wars of 1967 and 1973, which energized the Jewish communities of the Diaspora into strong support of Israel, and the continuing anti-Jewish campaign conducted by some of Israel's enemies have brought the Jewish state and the Jewish Diaspora closer together in the face of the common threat. Each nourishes the other, and a creative symbiosis has emerged since 1948.

Of course, Israel is developing its own unique national existence that is significantly different from Jewish life in the United States, Canada, South America, Western Europe, or the repressive Soviet Union. But the interdependence of Israel with the Diaspora remains a central reality of contemporary Jewish life. Yet that relationship is not without its ironies, one being that Jews as Jews are perhaps in greater physical danger in Israel than in the Diaspora. Five major wars since 1948 plus thousands of Arab terrorist attacks and the threat of future wars have been a fact of Israeli existence since the state was founded. Nor has an independent Jewish state ended the pathology of anti-Semitism in the world as Herzl and other Zionist leaders had hoped it would.

Over three hundred thousand Israelis, nearly ten percent of the current Israeli Jewish population, reside in the United States. Generally, Israelis living in the Diaspora are viewed negatively by those Jews who remain in Israel, but the expatriates form a potential human bridge of increased understanding between the Golah and the Jewish state. Despite all these problems, the creation of Israel in 1948 is one of the great events in Jewish history, ranking with the Exodus from ancient Egypt in its redemptive importance. Israel's independence, coming just three years after the end of the Holocaust, has stirred every Jew with pride and hope, and Israel has enriched the entire Diaspora in ways too numerous to list. And the Diaspora, for its part, has provided strength, sustenance, and solidarity for the people and the state of Israel. The Jews of Israel and the Jews of the Diaspora stand together as one indivisible people.

What are some appropriate roles for Christians who seek a just and lasting peace in the Middle East? What can Christians actually do to help achieve this deeply religious goal? If Christians truly seek to be peacemakers, what actions, programs, and policies should they undertake?

First, Christians should recognize that the core problem in the Arab-Israeli conflict is the Arab world's almost total unwillingness to accept a permanent, secure, and independent Jewish state in the Middle East. Only Egypt by its peace treaty with Israel has moved away from the basic Arab rejectionist position that refuses to recognize the legitimacy of Israel. Once the Arab world, especially the PLO, recognizes Israel, all other problems can be solved by negotiations including the rights of the Palestinian Arabs, the settlement of the Arab and Jewish refugee issue, and the status of Jerusalem. Once Western Christians understand this fact, they can, through their many contacts with the Arab world, become agents of reconciliation. Western Christians have an ongoing dialogue with their brothers and sisters in the Arab Christian churches, as well as with Arab Muslims. Instead of an uncritical acceptance of extreme Arab positions toward Israel, Western Christians should make every effort to change the Arabs' negative and ultimately self-defeating policy that denies to the Jewish people the same national rights the Arabs legitimately demand for themselves. Christian teaching materials, seminary training programs, sermons, liturgy, indeed, all of church life should reflect a respect for and an understanding of the realities of modern Israel— the state's origins and hopes as well as its problems and mistakes.

Christians should demand that the PLO publicly spell out what its stated goals really mean. Christians need to press the PLO leadership vigorously on the specifics of such oft-proclaimed phrases as "self-determination" and "legitimate rights." The PLO needs to know that Christians throughout the world will not accept its extremist and rejectionist aims toward Israel. If Christians do not demand that the Palestinian National Covenant be officially amended to recognize Israel, and if Christians do not call for an end to the PLO terrorist attacks on civilians, then Christians, even when well intentioned, are rendering a grave disservice to the cause of peace.

Christians would do well to follow the lead of French President François Mitterand who declared in Jerusalem during a 1982 state visit to Israel:

> How can the PLO, for example, which speaks in the name of fighters, hope to sit at the negotiating table as long as it denies the main thing for Israel, which is the right to exist and the means to maintain security? Dialogue presupposes mutual recognition of the other's right to exist, the mutual renunciation of direct or indirect warfare, it being understood that each regains his freedom of action in the case of failure.

President Mitterand's statement is similar to the American government's policy that rejects any contact with the PLO until the Palestinian group officially recognizes Israel and ends all acts of violence. The U.S. Catholic Conference has affirmed the right of Israel to live in peace as "a sovereign state with secure borders" as well as recognizing the Palestinian Arabs' right to a "homeland." The 1980 Middle East Policy Statement of the National Council of Churches also urged the PLO to recognize Israel and end all its "hostile acts." However, the NCC was sharply criticized by major Jewish organizations because, as the American Jewish Committee charged, the policy statement "endorses the concept of a PLO State to be established on the borders of Israel" and by so doing "contributes to the undermining" of the Camp David peace process.

Christians also need to be extremely careful that they do not employ a "double standard" when they judge Israeli actions and policies. There are many Christians in the West who support and even celebrate all of the many national liberation movements that have emerged since the end of World War II—all except one: Zionism. The double standard is also used when describing alleged Israeli human rights violations. Like every other state, Israel is imperfect in many areas of its national life, and as a democracy it readily acknowledges its shortcomings. But when Christians unfairly single out the

Jewish state alone in the Middle East for criticism, they weaken the professed Christian concern for justice and equity. The NCC Policy Statement warned against the temptation to scapegoat Israel:

> The National Council of Churches . . . recognizes the need to apply similar standards of judgment to all countries of the Middle East in questions of human or minority rights, and to resist singling out only one nation for particular focus without due recognition of other continuing human rights problems throughout the region.

Christians should also note the almost total absence of democratic freedoms in the Arab world, whether in monarchies like Jordan or Saudi Arabia, or in socialist states like Iraq, Syria, and Libya. Arab leaders often speak of how well Jews have fared within Arab societies, but Christians need to be acutely aware of the long record of anti-Jewish persecutions and excesses in those societies. Since 1948, ancient and once thriving Jewish communities in Arab lands have virtually ceased to exist except in Morocco. Following the creation of Israel, many Jews fled the Arab states, and those who remained have been periodically subjected to false arrests, anti-Semitic campaigns of vilification, expropriation of property, restrictions on travel, public hangings, and other cruel attacks. Jews, and Christians as well, have historically been second-class citizens in Muslim countries. As one Jewish refugee from an Arab country put it: "We were like tenants living in a Muslim-owned house. Now Israel is our own house, our own home."

The Israeli Labor Party dominated the nation's political life for twenty-nine years, from 1948 to 1977. Labor provided Israel's first five prime ministers: David Ben-Gurion, Moshe Sharett, Levi Eshkol, Golda Meir, and Yitzhak Rabin. But in 1977 and again in 1981, Labor was defeated by Menachem Begin's conservative Likud coalition. For Christians and Jews in the West who had become accustomed to Labor's long period of political control, Begin's election as Israeli prime minister was an unexpected jolt. Yet the Likud victories are a tribute to Israel's functioning democratic system, one that is sadly lacking in the neighboring Arab states. Begin's style and substance have upset many people in Israel and elsewhere. Still, Christians (and Jews) should carefully note that Israel, like the United States, is not a nation of dictatorial "maximum leaders," nor does

Israel have authoritarian "presidents for life" or autocratic "general-issimos." Rather, Israel has a thriving, often raucous, political system that has proven it can peacefully transfer power from one party to another without a *coup d'état*, martial law, assassinations, purge trials, or firing squads. Israel, like its American sister democracy, is a nation of laws and institutions, not of leadership personality cults.

Christians have every right to support or criticize the policies of any Israeli prime minister, as long as they are equally demanding of the Arab leaders and rulers. All political leaders come and go and are judged by God and history. Nations face the same judgment, but they do not come and go. They permanently survive because of their people and often in spite of their leaders. Legitimate disagreement with Begin or with any Israeli prime minister must not diminish support for Israel's right to survival as a Jewish state, particularly when its enemies are severely challenging that right every day.

Christians also have a moral obligation to repudiate publicly all acts of terrorism throughout the world. If terrorism is condoned or justified in one part of the world, the pathology will quickly spread, and innocent people become its victims. Here too a Christian double standard is sometimes at work. Armed Israeli responses to terrorism are widely condemned, but the PLO, which inspired and carried out the terrorist provocation, is often exempt from public censure. A policy of excusing the PLO is unfair, but, worst of all, such appeasement only encourages more terrorism in the future.

Christians should also publicly voice their objections to the Arab threats of a future oil embargo. Besides disrupting the world's energy supply, the embargo of 1973 and 1974, following the Yom Kippur War, actually devastated many of the fragile economies of the Third World countries of Asia, Africa, and South America. The industrialized West and Japan were financially hurt by the oil embargo, but the Third World peoples were plunged further into poverty and despair, first by the oil cutoff and then by the brutal inflationary rise in the cost of fuel. In an increasingly interdependent world, Christians should speak out against such economic warfare whose main victims are the poor and the hungry of the world.

Many people wonder why the Vatican does not have formal diplomatic relations with the state of Israel. Three explanations are usually cited. First, the Vatican does not recognize a state whose borders are not permanent and internationally accepted. For this reason, the Vatican does not maintain formal relations with the kingdom of Jordan either since its borders remain subject to negotiation. Second, the Vatican fears for the physical well-being and safety of the Christian population in the Arab countries. Finally, there is the theological question of the meaning of a reborn Jewish state for Christian thought and belief.

Many Catholic leaders, however, argue that with the enormously increased Christian understanding and appreciation of Jews and Judaism that has been gained since Vatican Council II, the theological objection is no longer valid. These leaders also note the many frequent and cordial contacts between Rome and Jerusalem. In 1973, Prime Minister Golda Meir met with Pope Paul VI, and two Israeli foreign ministers have also had papal meetings. At one of them, Pope John Paul II spoke of his concern for "the security of the state of Israel." The Vatican has also abandoned its previous call for the internationalization of Jerusalem; it now seeks "international guarantees" for the city. Current Vatican-Israeli relations have been described as "more than *de facto* and less than *de jure*," but Father Flannery believes it is time for the Vatican to fully recognize Israel: "The U.S. bishops should be among the foremost voices leading this cause."

Finally, Christians need to encourage continued U.S. support of Israel. As a nation America has made a profound moral commitment to Israel's survival and security, and every nationwide poll since 1948 has provided clear evidence that the overwhelming majority of the American public supports Israel in its struggle to survive. The American moral promise transcends political parties as well as religious, ethnic, and racial differences. This does not mean that America and Israel will not differ with each other, nor does this prevent American Christians and Jews from criticizing Israel, just as Israel is free to criticize U.S. policies and behavior. Good friends who are members of the same democratic family will always express their differences and disappointments as well as the esteem and affection they hold for each other. Justified criticism that is offered in respect and love by a friend is taken more seriously than when it comes from an adversary or enemy.

There are several specific programs that Christians can undertake to build friendship and trust with Israel and her people. First, Christians can acquaint themselves firsthand with Israel, the land and the people. Christians often receive inaccurate or incomplete information about the Jewish state from the media or from their own churches. The best way to overcome this problem is to visit Israel in person as part of a study-tour. Such journeys for peace and understanding may be church-sponsored or they may be interreligious in composition, bringing Christians and Jews together to gain a clearer insight into Israel. In the past such trips have proven to be unforgettable learning experiences for everyone concerned. The American Jewish Committee provides guidance and assistance in developing comprehensive study-tours to Israel.

There are many valid projects in Israel that merit Christian support. One of them is the "Interns for Peace" program that sends young American volunteers to Israel in a "Peace Corps" type effort. The interns provide badly needed social welfare assistance to Israeli Jews and Arabs in small towns and villages. Like millions of other people, members of the American Baptist Churches were stunned and saddened by the 1974 Palestinian Arab terrorist attack upon Israeli schoolchildren in the town of Maalot in Galilee. Sickened by the murderous actions of the terrorists, the American Baptist leadership sought a concrete way to build a sense of reconciliation between the Jews and Arabs of northern Israel. From the pain and suffering of the massacre has come an ABC-sponsored project of youth education involving the Jewish youngsters of Maalot and the Arab students of the neighboring village of Tarshisha.

One of the most remarkable projects in Israel is the Christian *moshav*, or collective settlement, of Nes Ammim, located north of the city of Acre near the Mediterranean coast. It was founded in the early 1960s by a Dutch Christian physician, Johan Pilon, who sought "to do something real" to express Christian solidarity with the Jews of Israel. Nes Ammim, which in Hebrew means a "sign unto the nations" (Isa. 11:10; 62:10), is a living community of one hundred fifty Christians from Holland, the U.S., Switzerland, West Germany, Sweden, Canada, and Britain. They do not missionize among the Jewish people but seek instead to work with the Israelis to develop the country. The moshav's leaders do not limit themselves to mere "sermons and songs," but are committed instead to actual service and labor. Nes Ammim's chief products are fresh flowers that are exported to Europe for sale.

The settlement's children attend Israeli schools, and the Shabbat (Saturday) is observed as the Christian Sabbath. Lectures and seminars on Christian-Jewish relations are a regular part of Nes Ammim's life. There is a modern guesthouse for the many visitors who come to visit the only Christian moshav in Israel. As Lev and Eve Bausch, the current leaders of Nes Ammim, told me: "We want to live in friendship with Israel. We want to turn over a new leaf in Christian-Jewish history. Christians have persecuted, expelled, and finally murdered Jews. Nes Ammim is our answer to that awful history. We live in dialogue with Jews. We are not missionaries to the Jewish people."

Nes Ammim is close to kibbutz Lohamei-Hagetaot, the ghetto fighters' community that was established after World War II by the survivors of the Polish and Lithuanian ghettos. At first, Nes Ammim's Jewish neighbors, victims of the Holocaust, were wary of the Christian moshav. They saw it as a subtle attempt to convert Jews to Christianity, but in time the people of Nes Ammim proved by word and deed that they were not missionaries. Relations soon improved, and today Nes Ammim is a welcome and respected member of the Western Galilee community. The American Friends of Nes Ammim has been organized to support Israel's Christian moshav.

Another important U.S. group is the National Christian Leadership Conference for Israel which brings together Roman Catholics, mainline Protestants, Evangelicals, and Orthodox Christians—clergy and lay, blacks and whites—"to take their stand with Israel and work for its just cause." The NCLCI through its many programs and publications promotes greater understanding of Israel within American churches. It also provides important information and interpretation about the Middle East, and the Conference's broad-based membership reflects the continuing American Christian support for Israel.

Within Israel itself there are many Christian organizations and institutions including the Evangelical Institute of Holy Land Studies on Mount Zion in Jerusalem that offers both undergraduate and graduate courses of instruction in Bible, Hebrew, history, and archaeology. The Ecumenical Institute for Theological Studies, located on the Jerusalem-Bethlehem road, is a center of advanced research. Other institutions include Isaiah House, founded by members of the Dominican Order; Baptist House; and the Ratisbonne Seminary—all in Jerusalem. There are also several interreligious groups in Tel Aviv and Jerusalem. The International Christian Embassy is also in Israel's capital city. The embassy is an independent evangelical institution whose members "love and honor the Jewish people."

Most of these groups maintain libraries, sponsor research projects, conduct services, lectures, and seminars, and publish journals and newsletters that deal with the Christian encounter with Jews, Judaism, and the state of Israel. These organizations and institutions generally welcome Christian visitors to Israel.

Israel has the potential to bring Jews and Christians closer together. The Jewish state can be a catalytic bridge between two great and ancient faith communities. Marc H. Tanenbaum, the American Jewish Committee's National Interreligious Affairs Director, sees an analogy in the way Jews are grappling with history in Israel and the way Christians have done so in Christian societies. Rabbi Tanenbaum has written:

> The land of Israel represents for the Jewish people the spatial center of Judaism. The experience of Christendom and Christianity's encounter with history and modernity which has taken place in a variety of spatial centers finds its analogies in the way in which Judaism is seeking to engage modernity and history in the land of Israel . . . the degree to which Jews are able to resolve the relationship in constructive ways . . . may have some instruction for others who are concerned about the present spiritual crisis for the whole of mankind.

Christians and Jews are both "prisoners of hope." In the quest for a just and lasting peace between Israel and its neighbors, people must not yield to despair, impatience, false optimism, or unrealistic pessimism. But together, armed with facts and faith, and with compassion and concern for all the peoples in the region, people can work to make a difference. A prayer of the synagogue might well be the guide for this crucial and life-affirming task: "Be strong, be very strong, and let us strengthen one another" in seeking peace and justice for Israel and its neighbors in the Middle East.

List of Sources

Antonius, George. *The Arab Awakening: The Story of the Arab National Movement.* Philadelphia: J. B. Lippincott, 1939.

Avineri, Shlomo. *The Making of Modern Zionism.* New York: Basic Books, 1981.

Baron, Salo W. *A Social and Religious History of the Jews.* New York: Columbia University Press, 1977.

Begin, Menachem. *The Revolt.* New York: H. Schuman, 1951.

Ben-Gurion, David. *Israel: A Personal History.* New York: Funk & Wagnalls Co., 1971.

Collins, Larry and Lapierre, Dominique. *O Jerusalem.* New York: Simon & Schuster, 1972.

Davidowicz, Lucy S. *The War Against the Jews: 1933–1945.* New York: Holt, Rinehart, & Winston, 1975.

Drinan, Robert F. *Honor the Promise: America's Commitment to Israel.* New York: Doubleday & Co., 1977.

Eban, Abba S. *My Country: The Story of Modern Israel.* New York: Random House, 1972.

Eckardt, Alice, and Eckardt, Roy A. *Encounter With Israel: A Challenge to Conscience.* New York: Association Press, 1970.

Eliav, Arie L. *Land of the Hart: Israelis, Arabs, the Territories, and a Vision of the Future.* Philadelphia: Jewish Publication Society, 1974.

Elon, Amos. *The Israelis: Founders and Sons.* New York: Holt, Rinehart, & Winston, 1971.

———. *Herzl.* New York: Holt, Rinehart, & Winston, 1975.

Fishman, Hertzel. *American Protestantism and a Jewish State.* Detroit: Wayne State University Press, 1973.

Gruen, George E., ed. *The Palestinians in Perspective.* New York: American Jewish Committee, 1982.

Halpern, Ben. *The Idea of the Jewish State.* Cambridge, Mass.: Harvard University Press, 1969.

Hertzberg, Arthur, ed. *The Zionist Idea: A Historical Analysis and Reader.* Garden City, N.Y.: Doubleday and Co., 1959.

Heschel, Abraham Joshua. *Israel: An Echo of Eternity.* New York: Farrar, Straus & Giroux, 1969.

141

Holtz, Avraham, ed. *The Holy City: Jews on Jerusalem.* New York: W. W. Norton & Co., 1971.

Katz, Samuel. *Battleground: Fact and Fantasy in Palestine.* New York: Bantam Books, 1973.

Laqueur, Walter. *A History of Zionism.* New York: Holt, Rinehart, & Winston, 1972.

——, ed. *The Israel-Arab Reader: A Documentary History of the Middle East Conflict.* New York: Bantam Books, 1971.

Lewis, Bernard. *The Arabs in History.* New York: Harper & Row, 1967.

Littell, Franklin H. *The Crucifixion of the Jews.* New York: Harper & Row, 1975.

Moskin, J. Robert. *Report From Jerusalem: City at the Crossroads.* New York: American Jewish Committee, 1977.

Parkes, James W. *Whose Land? A History of the Peoples of Palestine.* New York: Taplinger, 1970.

Peck, Abraham J., ed. *Jews and Christians After the Holocaust.* Philadelphia: Fortress Press, 1982.

Sachar, Howard M. *A History of Israel: From the Rise of Zionism to Our Time.* New York: Knopf, 1976.

Said, Edward W. *The Question of Palestine.* New York: Times Books, 1979.

Shapira, Avraham, ed. *The Seventh Day: Soldiers Talk About the Six Day War.* New York: Charles Scribner's Sons, 1970.

Spiro, Melford E. *Kibbutz: Venture in Utopia.* New York: Schocken Books, 1971.

Weizmann, Chaim. *Trial and Error: The Autobiography of Chaim Weizmann.* New York: Harper & Bros., 1949.

Index